Soul Resur

A Guide to Reincarnation

Poppy Palin

**Capall Bann
Publishing**

www.capallbann.co.uk

Soul Resurgence
A Guide to Reincarnation

©2000 Poppy Palin

ISBN 186163 116 2

Cover and internal illustrations by Poppy Palin
Cover design by Paul Mason

Published by:

Capall Bann Publishing
Freshfields
Chieveley
Berks
RG20 8TF

Acknowledgements

This book owes something to each of the following people:

Mark Austin, a brilliant teacher and a truly kind spirit.

Dave Kendall, for conversations past and future, a real visionary and questing soul.

Julia and Jon Day, for having the courage to get the ideas seen, in the world.

Rae and Ashley, for sharing their own bright visions and their inspirational words...we are not alone!

*"It's there to find if you have the mind
And you don't live in fear of it.."*

The Levellers, *Men-an-Tol*

About The Author

Poppy Palin is an artist and writer currently living in Warminster (once the UFO capital of Britain!) but is prone to Nomadic bursts! She is the author and illustrator of four books published by Capall Bann on her work as a Spirit Walker or Wildwitch. A professional Tattooist, Poppy combines art, writing and spiritual insights to express her own sacred way of being, whilst hoping to encourage others to do the same. Her latest project, 'The Wild Spirit Divination Cards', A Tarot of Nature, is well underway and more books on Spirit Walking are brewing in her creative cauldron! Poppy also writes fiction and in-between bouts of manic activity enjoys walking, singing and organic gardening (slowly!)

About the Artwork

The illustrations included in this book are from a series called Wildcraft. They represent the energy, life-force and spirit of the natural world, depicting ordinary people in harmony with themselves and others. The aim was to break the mould in terms of the usual drawings of impossibly perfect people, instead showing the vibrant diversity of human incarnate forms.

This book is dedicated to Mikey, without whom there would have been nowhere to write it! With my love and thanks to his beautiful spirit. May the Force be with him!

Other books by the author, also published by Capall Bann:

Season of Sorcery - On Becoming A Wisewoman

Wildwitch - The Craft of the Natural Psychic

Walking With Spirit - A Guide For the Natural Psychic

Contents

Foreword

There is, perhaps, only one guideline to live by...know thyself. By this, I do not mean know who you are in person. It is easy, for example, to know who Poppy Palin is. She is a writer, artist and psychic, these are good labels to hang upon her. However, I refer to knowing the SELF, the eternal essence inside the shell which bears your current name, in spirit. To know thyself in soul terms is to know the singularly most profound truth for all can be found within that beautiful and indestructible collection of energies that is your spirit. It is a unique and miraculous expression of the cosmos, a microcosm of the macrocosm, it is a reflection of the divine spark, of the Greater Spirit.

However, to know the soul is to first acknowledge its existence at the core of who you are today.

If this seems a little too much to contemplate (suddenly having to see yourself as all-powerful and everlasting when you'd happily delegated all that hard graft of being in charge to God!) then at least contemplate the possibility of your having a soul. Possibility and probability are all there are in this moment.

Nothing is permanent, nothing is certain in this fleshy material realm in which we currently dwell. All is change, spiral and circle in nature, and we are of nature, not above or apart from it. We rot like the animals, like the leaves. We die.

It is the contemplation of the possibility that we die in body only that allows us to consider that we can be born again....that we as a soul-essence can continue. What if that were true?

The healer/writer M.H. Tester says in the book *How to be Healthy, Wealthy and Wise* (Aquarian 1988) "When you reach the end of your life here you will cast off your body like a worn overcoat.....It may be at this moment that you cannot accept this truth. No matter. keep an open mind and read on. But while you are doing so, pause from time to time and consider. Consider your own immortality. You are immortal. You will survive this life. Get used to the idea. It changes everything!" To this I would add that it is only the possibility of soul surviving body that one may open up to in order to read this book. From there, the probability of reincarnation is easier to come by. Yet nothing is easy when one begins this brave and honest contemplation. With such possibilities and probabilities comes responsibility, not only to the eternal self but to the All from which that soul-self came.

This is a book for the seeker of personal truth who is not afraid to admit that to know is to fully understand and accept that we do not know. It is a book for the questing individual who is willing to go with the flow of the universe with integrity and honesty. It is a book of soul-poetry but only those with a brave heart may be moved to hear and feel the lyricism of the concept that we are eternal. Reincarnation is about soul dancing, soul resurgence, soul playing. But most of all it is about pure soul, unshackled from bodily bonds.

Can you accept the possibility or do you not wish to be aware of the dance? Both are feasible options, there is no right answer. But only one answer that will allow you to read on.

Introduction

We are one another.

With this simple line, taken from the great and groundbreaking work of the late Dr. Arthur Guirdham, we are given a key. This key is not to open the door to some part of the mysteries, to a fragment of the whole. This simple but profound sentence opens the floodgates to the whole boundless thing...to the essence of the All. If we are indeed one another then how may we feel hate, prejudice, fear? If we are one another then how may we lay blame or persecute, bully or manipulate? To do so to another is to harm the self.

That is, of course, if we give this line of thought any credence. Why should we? How on earth can we be one another? Aren't we all profoundly different? Isn't there evil and corruption and greed in the world? Are we not spiritually enlightened souls and how could we possibly be a part of that stuff out there...that nasty, destructive stuff? How could we possibly say that we are one another when there are rapists and murderers, liars, paedophiles and dictators in the universe?

To even begin to consider the truth that we are indeed in potential, in possibility, one another then we must ask another question.

Why are we here?

If you believe that we are here to evolve, to ascend, to become perfect and pure and entirely holy and if you actually would like this to happen then I suggest that you have bought into a male, patriarchal, western middle-class myth. Who on earth can make the standard of what is perfection and who could possibly legislate that there was a universal benchmark for such a state? God himself? If one discounts the notion that there is one supreme judge, who is a male figure of indeterminate values (save what mortal men have foisted upon his image) then we are left adrift. And adrift is where we should be. Because we are here to learn. That is our purpose. Not to become whiter than white and sin-free (if we revert to the idea that someone has passed judgement on what sin is). To learn we must be free of such rigid concepts as ascension.

We are here to learn, learning is a quest. To quest efficiently we must let go of the baggage and be willing to listen and to drop old, comforting ideas. I suppose that it is comforting to imagine that one has incarnated in order to become one of the ascended masters of the white light so championed by the new-age thinkers. This is fine if one happens to be an affluent Caucasian male. This concept applies in a similar guise in all leading monotheistic religions. Its okay for those Muslim men who are sin-free according to the Koran. Or to the Buddhist monks who shun the world in order to attain nirvana. What about the rest of us...the disadvantaged, the mentally sick or the disabled? What about the women? What about the tribes-people of colour? If perfection and ascension measured by one mans own fallible hand were true then what would be the point of incarnation for the millions of souls who currently inhabit other bodies than the chosen few?

"What just God would create some men wretched, and others happy and prosperous, if one life were all that they could have?" Marion Bradley, *The Mists of Avalon*, Sphere 1984.

No one learns in a state of fear, of value-judging others, of aggression towards some pre-determined enemy. Whose enemy? Think about all you receive daily from the media as truth, about the journalistic excitement garnered by pointing fingers, by demonising the unknown. Think about your history lessons, about your reading of facts placed before you. Think about your own received opinions and the consequent xenophobic tendencies they have seeded within you.

Now imagine encountering all that information again from this new perspective. We are one another. Think about the change and transformation of hate into compassion, distaste into empathy or sympathy, resentment into kindness. The magical act of imagination to actually perceive that could have been me gives a whole new spiritual and emotional perspective on the whole of creation.

There are no exceptions to this, we cannot exclude Peter Sutcliffe because we find his behaviour towards women unforgivable. Nor can we omit Myra Hindley because she goes against the maternal in an extreme way. We cannot rule out anyone from the possibility, infinitesimal though it may seem, that we could have been that way too. Hitler, Molosevic, Gadaffi, Saddam....all just as possible as Mother Teresa of Calcutta. All just as possible as the bloke down your road who wakes you up every Sunday with his lawn mower or his music.

You and I could be in their shoes today, or tomorrow, or yesterday, as time is cyclical not linear, after all....

If one can open up to this possibility then one may be able to consider reincarnation as a fact also....or at least, if not a fact at least a tool for understanding that key concept....I could have been them/him/her....we are, in potential, one another. You could have been born in any other body in any other place. A change in circumstance, a twist of fate, an unfortunate combination of events and we could be the murderer or the rapist. To consider this is to be open to kindness. To be truly spiritual is to be kind.

So, reincarnation. Not just this one incarnate life in the here and now but many. Many more than we could even consider. Some souls have just arrived, maybe with two or three lives behind them. Others have come back over centuries, have been through wars, religions, reigns of monarchs, from peasant to rich landowner and back to servant. These details are fascinating and, as we shall see, can be accessed by a simple technique....not as a day-tripper through time nor for entertainment, but to understand our souls pattern. We can access other lives and other selves but always from the perspective that we are one unique and eternal soul. We can observe our souls growth, its mistakes and its triumphs and its yearnings by looking into our past (other) lives.

I am eternal and cannot be destroyed,

I am a centre of thought and consciousness,

I am a centre of influence and power, I carry the divine spark within me,

I exist independent of my body,

My soul is eternal, part of the All,

My soul is invincible,

I AM.

We are all soul, soul wearing flesh. Flesh that can be presently a soldier, a thief or a business tycoon as easily as it can be a nurse, a charity worker or a mother. Flesh that can have male or female genitalia. Flesh which is temporary, it falls away after doing the job. It is the soul vehicle in which the soul learns lessons. The soul learns not in order to evolve to this pre-ordained God-head status, but to be the best it can be. To be itself and to find the finest, most profound, most integrous expression of that self. The soul is incarnate in flesh of its own choosing. It picks a mask to wear for this life in order to experience and to participate in acts which will facilitate understanding and promote soul growth. The purpose of reincarnation, of wearing a fleshy guise, of living a life in the manifest realm is fore the soul to grow and quest and to BECOME. The soul needs to grow as any organic thing does. It goes through periods of regeneration and resurgence and periods of sleep. Its role is to be the most beautiful and supreme expression of itself that it can be.

Each soul is a unique organism. Each soul aspires to its own perfection. Its own knowing and being. It may cease to incarnate when it has truly learned compassion and gained wisdom through experiencing what it is like to be many selves in many lives. The soul remains the same, of its type, unique and individual and the way it responds will be appropriate to its soul type. However, the guise, the flesh, the form and circumstance will be chosen out of life's dressing up box purely to facilitate this process. Flesh is weak, soul is strong. This is why, manifestly, we are one another. In order to learn how it is to be a woman, a black man, a Hindu or a blind person we may put on their bodily shell. If we believe that we have reason to hate such a person, to ridicule or ignore them in one life then we may chose, as a soul, to wear their mantle next time around. The soul, on the whole, wishes to grow. Sometimes it may be hurt or scarred or twisted by particularly cruel manifest lives. Burning at the stake, disembowelling, race annihilation...these are a few of the traumas that can wound beyond flesh and into the eternal soul. Soul is eternal, yes, but it can be temporarily hurt in its quest for self-improvement.

Does anyone oversee this constant role-playing of the souls? The answer is yes, in a gentle and loving way. Each soul is assigned a spirit Guide or mentor whose role it is to accompany the person through a part of or the whole of an incarnation. Guides may come and go but like belly buttons each incarnate human soul has a Guide. It is entirely up to us if we tune into them or not. Again, the simple and effective techniques for this will be discussed in the text. However, as we have such a valuable spiritual friend who is uniquely ours (as they are attuned to our essential unique soul type, residing in our physical shells) it seems folly not to commune with them.

From wide personal experience I can say that the Guide is utterly and totally priceless. It is they alone who can give one a cosmic and spiritual overview as they are removed from human emotional involvement and short-sightedness. It is they who can show one parts of the vast links and webs and connectedness between all souls. No soul goes through incarnation alone as even our smallest actions have far-reaching consequences. For example, if we grumpily ignore the man at the bus stop one rainy day then he takes this personally and is rude to his secretary in the office who then is angry with him and so passes this on to her children that evening who then make a mess of their homework...and so on. Think of the grander scale this is on over incarnations...the repercussions of the soul for the murderer to the murdered, the tormented child to the abusive father....

No soul can claim immunity from others or isolation from the All. We are indeed one another, our actions spreading out to influence across miles and across incarnations. Lovers seeking lovers across the centuries, old scores to be settled, lessons to be learned and old scenarios to be played out in order to learn. One soul may wish to see you even if you have no wish to meet that soul again. The Guide can help and, indeed, guide the individual soul as to why things are happening in this incarnation. They also aid the process of love, compassion and understanding of others by revealing to the soul why others may be wounded enough to behave in inappropriate ways.

As a writer and speaker on the topic of psychic questing and reincarnation I hope to answer some of the more frequently asked questions about this vast, fascinating and complex subject. As I consider the matter of reincarnation to be central, a core element of our being, then I shall be explaining this strongly held system of belief by using actual examples of those who have encountered their other lives and alternate selves. I will be devoting a chapter to the concept of soul type, soul group and soul mate, areas which often confuse or intrigue many questing folk. Ultimately I will be showing how I believe a working knowledge of some, if not all, of our other lives can be a valuable tool in under-standing the essential soul-self. Such soul-work can shed light on relationships, career, children and patterns and problems in any area of incarnate life. With a disciplined and respectful attitude, anyone can be empowered to do such inner-work themselves.

Soul Resurgence sets out to show that 'we are one another' is one of the most spiritually liberating and uplifting concepts when explained through the paradigm of reincarnation.

If one allows the idea that time is only linear by man's making then one can no longer refer only to past lives, simply to other lives and different selves....truly a reflection of our interconnectedness on manifest and soul levels.

Poppy Palin,
Wiltshire, 1999.

Chapter One

In the Beginning.....

There was soul.

It did not have red hair and freckles, it wasn't good at chess, it wasn't called Lynn or Ed or Sandy. It just was. Hard to imagine? Do we need visual clues to be able to picture a concept? If, as John Lennon suggested, God is a concept by which we measure our pain then perhaps soul is a concept by which and from which we can measure....everything. Too big to contemplate? Then let us get back to basics.

Where do you consider yourself to be inside your body?

At which point can you feel a swell of consciousness, the point where you feel you dwell, that bit of you that is reading or thinking right now? If you cannot get a sense of self within the framework of the body then let me share with you the most common feeling that other people have, including myself. The general answer to this is that people feel that they dwell somewhere just above, but between, their human eyes. The middle of the forehead. Although it is technically impossible to actually physically see from this point (without extensive physical modification!) there is a sense of sight and of being in the space between the actual eyes. Thus it is widely known as the third eye, minds eye or psychic centre.

Poppy Palin

It is acknowledged as a chakra or energy centre on the body and as such is man area which requires protection. Although your soul occupies the entire body, its most direct point of contact is this third eye point.

If you cannot feel a place where you seem to be inside your body then spend a little time imagining you are located at this very spot within yourself. When you achieve a sense of place then turn your attentions to how this sense of 'you-ness' appears. As human beings we need a clue or two to be able to picture something. So once you have located your soul inside then perhaps it suggests a shape or a colour or a smell to your actual bodily self. The image that comes most readily to me is a bright glass jewel such as one I had as a child which I took to be very precious and valuable. Its cut facets reflected a myriad of amazing colours. This I see at my third eye with those bright sunlit rays of almost impossible colours radiating down throughout my body. I cannot see my soul as any more solid than that. I cannot see a human shaped gaseous cloud. But maybe you can? It is, as with all things psychic and spiritual, advisable to go on the first impression that one receives, no matter how mad it may appear . Try to quash the logical rational self for a moment (it has enough to do day to day, give it a break!). Go with whatever you see initially, be this a vapour or a pink-tinged steam, a crystal or a shining star.

Why this need to visualise soul? So that we may discuss its origins and journeys with more than a feeling of bewilderment. We cannot put familiar dressings upon soul to recognise it. Soul is pure raw life energy. It does not need a moustache or a pair of designer jeans for its life outside the incarnate bodily realms. It can be recognised and worked with as it is in spirit. So it helps us if we have a human notion of this energy. One cannot really visualise air but it is possible to visualise the thrumming of an energy making that air vibrate. If you prefer to see soul as an amorphous mass of humming air then this is good, if it becomes a rainbow or a swirling mist this is fine too. But embodying a soul with human attributes, the likes of which it only needs as a vehicle to travel in on earth, will hamper out pure understanding of the energy involved.

So, what am I suggesting here? That your deceased Aunt Jean or your childhood pet dog do not look like themselves now they have passed over? How on earth could we recognise our loved ones in spirit if they no longer resemble the people or creatures we knew? I am suggesting that spirit may, and often does, don a familiar guise when it visits us. This visit may be a psychic communication, it may be the collection of someone who is dying here on earth, it may be the appearance in meditation as a Guide or Guardian Angel. The old bodily set of clothes may be worn to help a human soul through the transition stage between life and the Other Realms, especially if the person is afraid or strictly unspiritual by earthly incarnate nature. But spirit or soul in the Otherworlds is as it is, unadorned and free of the restrictions of bodily need or impairment.

This may be scary stuff and unfamiliar in the extreme. Weren't we all taught about some variation on the theme of heaven where our ancestors paraded round looking...well, that bit was always a tad ambiguous! The ages and appearances of the dead in this uniformly wondrous place caused a few questions to be asked by even the smallest curious child. What if your Mum died at an earlier age than you yourself died. Did that mean in heaven that you were older than your mum for all eternity? How very odd! Did man who lost a leg in Vietnam grow it back in heaven or did he never get there anyway? Was there a place in paradise for a soldier who had killed? And so it goes on when we deal with this familiar but utterly limiting and naive construct. The old way of looking at the afterlife is comforting but fraught with spiritual potholes to catch to astral cyclist unawares. The other way of considering the soul in its eternal state is disturbing at worst, confusing at best. But it makes consistent sense if one can drop the need for human guises.

Nobody knows whether the Otherworld has houses or clothes or the need for either. I do not claim to know. I suggest that because we chose to live in such a manner whilst incarnate, due to the elements upon this planet, then we find it hard to imagine or indeed visualise a life without them. However, I believe it to be much more appropriate to put forward the idea that the discarnate human soul does not require creature comforts. It derives its comfort and its security in the vastness of existence in boundless time (outside of human delineations) with other energies of its type. It reunites with soul groups, soul-mates, kindred spirits. These spirits may have worn many guises throughout incarnations but it would be impossible to imagine them needing to be recognised as both an Egyptian slave and a Italian architect all at once. In spirit, there is no need for the flamboyant costumes, stereotypical roles or masks that we have to don in bodily life in order to play at being other characters in a variety of settings. In spirit we recognise our soul family by the vibration of love. As with any universal principle or force, soul is energy with a frequency. Soul cleaves to soul by a response to this unique and pure pattern of energy waves. Then soul reunites with soul to pool the collective and individual learning that has taken place on earth. I see no need for discarnate soul to do this over a cup of virtual tea in a replica of a manifest dwelling!

I have come across such a conglomeration of energies, a cloud of spirit, whilst obtaining guidance from the Otherworlds. As a natural psychic, it is possible to sit in a relaxed (but astrally protected) state and access any energy or life force that is willing to communicate. This particular mass of spiritual power, a 'nest' of souls who were obviously well travelled together, made me feel uneasy at first. The guidance that this group passed on to me was just as valid as any other piece of information I have ever received from spirit. Yet because I was used to souls donning the guises of men or women I felt somewhat disconcerted by the concept of souls mingled together as one vast miasma. Where was the sense of the individual in that? Where we all destined to lose out selves in the envelopment of other more dominant spirits? Not at all! The group were as inextricably linked as they could be but were also able to separate. They chose not to...there was choice and free will, in accordance to the natural way of things. They also had chosen to fragment in order for much learning to be done by the group as a whole. If it sent five souls to incarnate whilst five more stayed in spirit to guide them then the learning that occurred was far greater and more beneficial en masse and so to the universe.

As individual souls, as single sources of pure energy, expressing itself in a unique way, we still came from a composite soul group. We are of a soul type. Again, this fits with the patterns of nature, everything belonging to a species or genus. As with the way of evolution, nature being in a constant state of change and adaptation, we split like cells from a single cell organism in the primordial soup. In order for the composite to develop, it sent out its individual representatives to gather different aspects of experience.

Put this way, the whole concept of groups of souls becomes less like an enveloping of individualism and more of a very organic way of promoting growth most effectively. As we are referring here to spirit, the model represents spiritual growth. But spirit, be it an etheric mist or an essence, is still part of the natural order. It is of the cosmos, a cosmos in which energy is all there is, energy expressed as solid, liquid or gas. Spirit is a gaseous liquid, perhaps, a shifting but quantifiable force. Some sensitive or psychic humans perceive this tangibly. Yet it is not a solid. The solid is the form that is enters in order to experience. Experience is the point of incarnating into the manifest. Experiencing in order for the root soul group or species to learn and grow.

The point of evolving from and belonging to a soul species does not mean that there is a hierarchy. With reference to the natural manifest world, how can one deem the species of dog better or worse than the species of cat? How can one define Mars as being better than Venus? One can say that the dog has certain qualities or that Mars has certain attributes but it is not feasible to say that one is superior. We as souls or as incarnate beings have preferences due to either soul type or to incarnate experience (two different things). The lesson from this knowledge of preference is that preferring something does not make it universally superior or supreme...only more appropriate to the self. As an example, the difference between the man who claims all modern pop music is rubbish and the woman who expresses the opinion that some of it could be considered technically good but it is not to her taste.

So, then, the nature of the discarnate human entity...the soul....is to be an individual expression of a collective feeling or energy. The individual soul may incarnate with the same souls from its group over and over, or it may have one special partner from the collective with which it acts out its dramas on the earth. This is the soul-mate relationship...not always the comfortable one we aspire to. The soul-mate relationship (and we may have many such scenarios with different souls as we evolve beyond one soul-mate link) is one which facilitates growth. If we were meant to curl up in a lovey dovey state of perfection for a whole life on earth then we may as well have stayed in spirit where love is the natural state of being and all is at peace. Life isn't a reflection of this bliss-state. The soul-mate scenario isn't always the partner/lover one. It can be best friend, father, sister... any one in between. It can even be a rival or adversary that somehow we feel bonded to. It is a key and important relationship, for sure, but it is one with a member of our soul group who we recognise on some level and who we can work well with in the learning game.

The soul-mate dilemma/idyll is one that the majority of western adults will have encountered for themselves. However, this is usually accepted to be within the context of a loving partnership, be that heterosexual or no. The soul-mate in question more often than not feels familiar. A sensation of having known each other for years occurs almost immediately. That electrical charge of recognition which has little to do with sexual attraction (but is often interpreted as such) is the magnetic connection between two souls from the same collective of energies.

The soul-mate may indeed be one such soul from the group amalgam of kindred energies with which it has been agreed that a union on the earth plane will be beneficial. As it has already been suggested that such marvellous and immaculate relationships achieve little in this learning realm, it is unlikely that this overwhelming bliss of recognition will last. More often than not, this union can turn out to be one of testing, heartbreaking and traumatic proportions. This is due to the nature of that strong connection and how those powerful feelings react when faced with normal human situations, problems, hang-ups etc. This is where the mutual learning and growth take place. Sometime, this is hard for the individuals involved to comprehend...they meet their soul love only to be torn apart by it?

The logic of this is profound when one opens up to the possibilities of this as a true opportunity for spiritual growth. We as human beings will only learn truly on a deep level if we are dealing with strong, overwhelming emotions. Those trivial or passing acquaintances who test us will not make so much impression as the lover we adore....or in other (less recognised) soul-mate scenarios, the father or sister we adore. With a soul not of our type we may be tempted to say "sod it!" when the going gets tough and bail out of the situation without grasping any of the meaning of the lessons involved. The soul-mate or soul bond scenarios that shape our lives are those by which we carry our valuable soul lessons back to the group after our passing from this particular incarnation.

Sometimes, if we have chosen a bleak or very unstable incarnation for ourselves, then we may meet such a soul love for a short while as a means of touching base with something calm, loving and familiar. We may be surprised when the bringer of such love and comfort then moves on again but if we can understand that this life will pass away and that the purpose of hard times has already been agreed to by the souls involved then it is not so incomprehensible. "Tis better to have loved and lost than never to have loved at all" relates well to this. In a particularly gruelling or trying life on earth the soul-mate may pass through your life to give you the equivalent of an astral hug, reminding you subconscious, your soul level, what awaits you after bodily death. This could be seen as the equivalent of an astral "keep your chin up" piece of encouragement. When the going gets tough in life those with this sort of understanding will find strength to carry on. With this understanding it is easier to perceive that this is why some profound relationships seem to end when they seemed so perfect. They were there only as a reminder of the rewards to be reaped after the struggle of incarnation is over once more.

There is no way that such a perfect and Otherworldly soul partnership could survive modern life...even if the candidates were millionaires who could live in perfect isolation from modern western pressures. The validity of having met and lost such a love is not that we mourn the loss of the only perfect thing in the whole rotten world. It is that we have felt love that is the love that exists for us in spirit. Truly, to have had a soul partnership in life is a blessing and no matter how long it lasted and how badly it may have ended, to feel that level of soul connection on earth is indeed a gift and should be looked on as such, with thanks. That applies even if the person you felt so strongly for left you/was unfaithful/stole your money/was a secret addict. It also applies if your feelings rose to a level were they may have been interpreted as hate. Remember, soul-mate scenarios can be entirely gruesome or brief and spectacular. They are not mundane, but profound. They are the things we remember. Life changing and circumstance altering events. They are what life is all about.

Looking at the nature of the soul-mate link brings us to more knotty issues that usually surround this issue. Firstly, how many soul-mates can anyone have? Well, this reflects back on the old, tried and tested notion that we were all given as the answer. This option was that a fabulous Heaven was the only conclusion at the end of this, our one crack at life. So, let us open up to new possibilities and question this narrow and restricted vision. I remember a friend with a very Catholic perspective becoming quite vexed over the notion that if a woman's husband died and she then remarried and subsequently they both died, wouldn't it be awful when those two husbands met in heaven? I tried to look at this from her perspective. I could tell that she believed that we only had one true soul-mate in life who was hand picked for you by a God above and then you married them...nice and easy. Then, this impostor came along who wasn't as valid as husband number one. But where did he stand in relation to the wife in heaven?

This whole view of the afterlife simply does not work. Unless one entirely removes the human qualities (the mask/personality/gender/appearance) of the soul when it is out of the bodily realm then things become rather farcical. As we have seen, a newly departed soul may need the comfort of seeing relations dressed and looking as they did in order to comfort them into accepting the spiritual realms. However, these guises do not get maintained, unless a soul becomes entirely stuck close to the earth realm. This is not a common occurrence as most Guides/Guardians move these souls on. Yet it does happen, especially if the passing was unexpected or violent. Most ghosts are simply atmospheric tape/video recordings of events stored by buildings in their energy matrix...again, especially if the event that was recorded was profound or emotional. Soul does not need to hang around earth in fancy dress. Nor does it need to fret over who its earthly husband was. Soul cannot, as we have discussed, maintain all of its earthly guises after death. Most souls have incarnated many times and their persona, their earth trappings, get left behind with the redundant soul-vehicle...their dead human body. In the Otherworld there are, therefore, no husbands and wives.

Secondly, soul is neither male nor female, old nor young. (Although some souls have incarnated hundreds of times and can be classed as old souls accordingly, old hands at incarnating! They are old in terms of wisdom because of such experience. Often incarnation into a hostile world can be a great sacrifice leaving the peace and love of the astral realms and such souls take on these tasks on behalf of the group.) Because soul is naturally capable of incarnating into any sort of body, Asian, male, disabled, mentally ill...whatever combination the lessons of the life needs...then the male-female polarity bond is of no real relevance. Hence why the soul-mate scenario can be sister-sister or son-father. Hence also why you can believe that you have met one soul-mate in your partner, only to consider that your mother is a soul-mate too. I know of one man who does consider his mother to be a soul-mate although he has the insight not to consider her the only one.

We are not all boxed up in couples in the Otherworld. That is an invention of the Earth plane and not a very successful one. It keeps us all in splendid isolation in western society, dwelling in our little homes, oblivious of our neighbours woes, jealous of our possessions. Soul-mates are taken from the soul group. Therefore they can be many and various. Or you may meet none at all in an incarnation, although this is unlikely. Unlikely, but not impossible, nothing in spirit is to be ruled out in such a way. Yet why would a soul not meet anyone from their group in a lifetime? Well, to touch on a subject that will be returned to later, other souls can have a passionate need to see you and to work out lessons with you over and over again. To you, they may be of little consequence, but in their learning plan they may need to recompense you or learn to forgive you ...any number of variations on a theme. You may not recall their soul or deeds at all. You may not even register their presence around you!

This scenario is rare, as most groups of souls incarnate over and over and work with each other, loosely banded although there may be tenuous links between them. Currently, to my understanding, there are millions of souls incarnate who went through the Nazi holocaust together. Some of these souls were incidental and part of other groups who just learned that lesson from being there at the time. Other souls involved are part of a tightly knit (but loosely bonded in manifest terms) collective who have suffered many persecutions... the witch trial madness as an example.... together. Their returning is to share and learn about forgiveness. This is a large and ambitious task, one which involves probable lifetimes in the future, as well as in the now, to deal with. The resonance of such genocide lingers long in soul. Soul scars such as these bond the collective energies together in Otherworldly terms. Immense strength is gained in this way, the likes of which would not be achieved in a husband-wife in heaven, Hitler-in-hell, black and white understanding of the universe. We bond in groups, we have many soul links and maybe a few really close connections within the group but there is a much more unselfish and broad understanding of love and team work in soul terms as opposed to our insecure and fearful earthly way.

So, the nature of the discarnate human entity, the essence of us that resides in the soul vehicle (body) is eternal and sexless (with the capability of assuming any guise in bodily form). It is part of a group which collects by the type of energies it has. We will look at the relationship between soul type and earthly personality later. For now, it can be observed that these inherent soul energies, the essential vibration of soul which can evolve but not change fundamentally, are of a particular blend. These may be soul types which resonate to a particularly creative vibration who would successfully incarnate as great communicators by artistic or written means. The vibration may be more inclined to philosophy, invention, nurturing or any combination of these aspects of being. The types are broad and all-encompassing...not as limiting as they become in manifest expression.

A vibration may only be observed as a feeling. It is this general and overall feeling which determines which soul type our own spirit is akin to. It is this feeling which allows us to recognise something in the feel of a strangers vibration. The essence of this vibration is often noted in the persons eyes, the closest be can get to connecting with their third eye. These windows to the soul communicate without words the greater feel of our essential pure, raw essence...not just our physical differences. Few of us could deny ever having experienced this instant connection, be that with a positive or negative response. One can attribute those instant and unshakeable reactions to total strangers... "I just didn't take to him/her", "They didn't like me, I could tell", "I just warmed to them immediately". This has little to do with clothes, manner or looks. This is the soul in direct communication with other souls/soul types. The observation of such interaction in a social context is a valuable way to practically understanding this concept.

To end this chapter I will use another quote from the late songwriter and visionary, John Lennon. When Lennon wrote "Imagine there's no heaven, its easy if you try...." he was offering the listener to broaden their horizons a little, just by imagining. Which is the same principle I have used here, using the term possibility. Imagine the possibility of eternal soul, of that spark across the stars, across time and space which is uniquely yours. That is what this section has been, in essence.

To add, as a final illustration of this point using Lennon, his original "Imagine" idea came from his partner, Yoko Ono, who used her mind-expanding concept art in 'word-pieces'. These pieces were also designed to allow the observer to consider new and often strange possibilities. It was Yoko who became seen as John's soul-mate, one who was perceived by the public in the late nineteen sixties as highly unsuitable for their favourite pop star. What could John Lennon, millionaire genius, see in a little, wacky, unconventional Japanese woman? We know what he saw. He saw soul connection, through the eyes. He felt their link and he would have even if Yoko had been the size of a Sumo or badly disfigured by burns or any number of other variations on supposedly "undesirable" themes. They were of the same soul type. Lennon also found this soul link with Stuart Sutcliffe, the original Beatles bass player, a brilliant artist who died tragically young. Lennon had a male soul-mate too.

Can you perceive your own soul inside your bodily shell? What does it appear to you as? Can you recall connecting with another similar (or indeed different) soul type on sight (connection through the eyes)? Can you consider the possibility of this souls learning journey through the cycles of existence?

If so, we can go on to look at the purpose of this journey... reincarnation.

Chapter Two

The ABC of Soul Learning...The Purpose of Incarnation

Why does the soul need to incarnate at all when it seems to have a nice cosy lot in the Otherworld? Why doesn't it just hang around with its companion spirits in a pleasant, blissed-out state? As we can observe from nature, nothing is ever this static. Even if it takes millions of earth years to evolve, natural organisms will change, albeit so slowly that the adaptation is almost imperceptible. Sometimes in the natural world there are cataclysmic events which throw the status quo into turmoil but generally things in nature move onwards in a constant flow. As soul is raw energy and nature is based upon energy, from universal to individual, everything being made of energy made into matter, then it follows natures rules.

Soul needs to evolve, shift, change, grow. To be the best soul it can be, given its type. Nature has no blanket code of perfection. No one creature is deemed better than the other, maybe more adaptable, maybe more intelligent, maybe faster but never more perfect. Perfection on a grand, all-encompassing scale is not natures way. "Vive le difference!" is natures glorious rallying cry, with each particular creature or plant striving for its own best way of being. The individual also strives for this way as to benefit its group species and to ensure its survival. So the soul strives to benefit the way of the All.

As a part of the natural order, the old model of good/evil, black/white makes little sense. This rigid view which labels the exact definition of perfection is the cause of misunderstanding, fear, superiority and inferiority complexes...leading to war, extermination and hatred. It simply is not feasible as a way of perceiving the world and nature as a whole. At its most basic, this becomes black is dirty, white is clean and pure, and it doesn't take a great leap of consciousness to see where that little standard has got the human race. Similarly, this all-encompassing view of perfection or desirability has to come from one fallible human viewpoint. As God has not made himself manifest to the masses on a regular basis to lay down the universal law then we can only look to flawed human souls to tell us how it is. Man made rules exclude, delude and cause pain. They also throw up knotty and unanswerable questions.

For example, when a believer in the heaven concept is asked about whether Gandhi would be allowed in to this Christian place they are stumped. If Gandhi wasn't a good Christian then he couldn't be allowed access to paradise. Yet if he was a good soul/person how could he go to the Hell place with the likes of Hitler? Calling the shots on a code of good/perfection is down to the individual, it cannot be applied world-wide. It is subjective and as such is subject to human flaws and misconceptions. It is open to ignorance and judgement...two things which cause destruction of any perceived enemy by this delineation of good/evil.

I have recently observed a movement of people, self-proclaimed spiritual souls, who as the Christian millennium approaches claim that the world is somehow splitting into two factions. The good souls will somehow club together in one area whilst the bad souls will all have to fight it out elsewhere. The good are those who have apparently dealt with all of their problems and are ready to stop incarnating and ascend to perfection. The bad are those who will not clear their past debts in karmic terms, those who cling onto manifest sins such as greed or violence. There are variations on this theme. The good will be carried off in space ships whilst the bad stay on an earth which goes into spasm, tilts off its axis and becomes hostile to its inhabitants...

Woah there! Does this seem real to you? Can you honestly see one great hand of universal judgement being able to neatly separate the goodies and the baddies? Can you honestly see this being able to be done so neatly? Indeed, do you look at yourself incarnate and see an entirely good or bad person? Of course not! You are, as we all are, without exception. We are imperfect and striving to be improved. Not washed whiter than white. Improved. To improve is to become better at being the soul we inherently are by nature. That is all. To expand on this is to buy directly into the Aryan fantasies of Hitler or the slave trader mentality. No one soul is above or below. No one soul is black or white. We are talking about soul, not these temporary fleshy vehicles in which we dwell.

We all have these aspects within ourselves as incarnate souls, or we could not be incarnate. We are here to experience different views, different circumstances. We may needs to learn through experiences with money, learn to forgo material greed by actually feeling that greed. We may hurt others by our actions, we may even kill because we needed to go through that set of emotional and physical traumas. We may end up on Death Row because we were born poor and black and mentally ill. We may use chemical fertilisers, we may cause damage to property. We are here to learn and nobody learns anything by sitting back, arms folded, setting themselves apart from things thinking they are somehow absolved and above it. We are here to learn our connection to everything, we are not here to separate ourselves from all this nasty stuff and wait for ascension.

If there is no universal judging hand (and how can there be but one way of dealing with the human condition so neatly?) then we have nothing to fear. It the vast cycles of life and death and life there can be only one code to try and maintain. 'Do as you would be done by', 'if it harms none then do as you will',' love thy neighbour as you would yourself', 'respect for all life is the foundation'...however it is worded the message is the same. But the operative word is try. We try and be integrous, moral, kind and spiritual beings but we are in fallible human shells living in testing times. Therefore, the notion of being incarnate in order to rise above incarnation is rather pointless.

We are not armchair spectators to the follys of others. We can 'tut tut' at the news and emotionally distance ourselves from alarming, disturbing pictures of war and famine in miniature on the screen but we cannot delude ourselves that we are no a part of it. Certainly, we may not be directly responsible for the actions of one man in a distant land but we cannot call him evil and demonise him either. Not until we have walked in his shoes, seen and felt as he does, experienced his hurt or his ignorance.

We as different souls may have seen differently from his eyes, but being born into his circumstances may still have made us experience some of the anger and pain that makes him a warmonger. He is but a soul. He is a fellow soul, experiencing what he has chosen to, with other souls who have chosen their own paths. Yes, there is always free will.

Nobody need harm or maim or repress. Yet without these lessons of how not to behave, without feeling that outrage and disgust, how would we develop our own individual moral integrity?

I recently attended a spiritualist circle at which a duo of mediums were channelling spirit. The audience were required to ask questions of these two. One of the questions was, why is there still war if we are supposedly in (or entering into) a new age filled with enlightenment and peace? The answer from spirit was one which explored the same paradigm that I am sharing here. If there was no conflict there would be no growth or understanding. If there were no different view points or attitudes to be either respected or misunderstood (the choice is purely an individual one) then there would be no expansion of the souls knowledge or repertoire.

Similarly, when attending a writers workshop, the lecturer used the same analogy for the definition of a good book. Looking at incarnation as but a chapter in a good book makes us understand the need for conflict. Conflict keeps us turning the pages to see the characters response to adversity. We, as souls, are playing out our character roles in our chosen human shells. If we allow for the concept of reincarnation and consider its possibilities then we can see that this is all we are doing. Making mistakes really is not the end of the world and this goes for other peoples mistakes and misconceptions too. How would we understand our own souls definition of integrity if we did not have examples of what felt wrong?

Nobody decries the lion as an evil creature for killing the gazelle. It needs to live, that is what lions do, naturally. Nobody chastises the blackbird for tearing apart the worms, it is what she does. In certain circumstances, cases of extreme poverty, abuse, neglect and cruelty, souls incarnate do what they do, not out of an inherent evil but as an uninformed and instinctive reaction. As soon as a person claims that they could never rape/kill/lie/steal from a point of view of superiority rather than compassion then they themselves will be destined to experience an incarnation with circumstances which test their resolve. If one responds as a loving and sensitive soul and could never murder or abuse from the point of view of understanding the web of grief and agony that spreads out from one such action then the lesson is learned. It is the cries of 'evil' and 'bastard' that mean that the soul has not understood the patterns and roles that all souls can play out. Again, there are no exceptions. We are all capable as souls in bodies of committing crimes against nature. Capable of any action, positive or damaging. We must see this. This is why we incarnate.

Part of this understanding of incarnation is a grasp of how we affect the All. We have already touched on the concept of soul groups and types. These groups all come from the same root family...the energy of soul...and so are inextricably linked, though separate, rather like petals on a flower. The centre of the flower around which this myriad of petals cluster is the source. I call this Great Spirit, using the genderless, all-encompassing and compassionate Native American terminology. This is the energy centre of soul, the place of absolute love and beauty from which the souls radiate. This centre is the power pack of the universe, from which all things come and to which all things return. It is sexless, non-judgemental, pure energy. It does not need a personality, its response is the ultimate transmission of feeling through vibration.

How do I know this? I know that I do not know. Yet I feel able to state this as a possibility. To me it is a probability as it works on the principle of energy as does the universe and nature. It is a symbol of the generator of electricity of life. Nothing becomes animated without the power. I relate this directly to the microcosm of our own experience, be it scientific or basic. Some of us understand complicated circuitry while others of us feel the electrical charge in the air before a storm. In the macrocosm of the All, it then reflects out that such illuminating and profound power should be the source of the cosmic charge of life. Everything is related, be it large or small scale. This is the whole point, be that hypothesis or ultimate truth. We are all connected by energy and that energy must, by logic, have a source.

Within our soul collectives we are linked by our experiences and by our kindred natures. We are linked to a lesser degree to the other soul groups with whom we cross reference when we are incarnate. This linking can be experienced on the manifest levels by standing still on a crowed street, try Oxford Street in London on a summer Saturday afternoon and see how many of the strangers pass you by without you hardly registering their features or presence. How many do you recall, how many make you stare, how many remind you of someone else? This is an example of soul grouping at work. We pick out those we may feel akin to, although we do not know them at all, and we barely notice the rest although we are still touched by them. We breathe their air, brush by their skin, may pick up something that they drop and make them happy by handing it back.

We are connected to all soul groups to a lesser or greater extent. We are all linked and linked again. Therefore none of our actions is isolation. That dropped wristwatch that you pick up and hand back to the stranger will make them so happy that they go and buy their mother some flowers, a mother who was feeling very depressed who then cheers up and goes out to bingo where she wins a prize. That prize money sees her taking out some friends for lunch, one of whom then meets a man at the next table who falls in love with her...and so on. Nothing is isolated, everything is connected, everything is energies. Incarnate or in soul, that life force energy is the factor which links us. We may never meet the man who fell in love with the friend of the mother but we are still connected to him.

To be incarnate is to understand how connected we truly are. This works in two ways. Firstly, we are connected by soul group to those who we wish to meet again, to work with them on life's lessons, as we work well with them. This also applies to those who are of other soul types who either drift through the patterns of our lives as incidental but relevant bit part players, or those who feel that they would work well with your soul type to sort out an old, difficult problem. These deep soul links are profound on a subconscious level but not everyone is aware, beyond the nagging feeling of familiarity or dislike, that these are souls that we know. As a psychic or sensitive, it is very easy to spot the souls behind the role playing masks of their human incarnate persona. As a non-sensitive it is possible to access this information through work which we will discuss later.

Secondly, the understanding of the interconnected aspect of all life, animal, vegetable and mineral, is vital. With the beautiful adage of the gentle current of air caused by a flapping butterflies wings in Asia causing a storm over the Atlantic we can understand how no action occurs in isolation. We may not be directly responsible for another human beings actions, as we have stated, but we are not apart from them as they will effect us. Similarly our own actions affect the All in an endless and surprising way. Reaping what you sow could be applied to this and the energies we put out into the world will rebound and be felt by us in equal measures in other ways. Thought is an energy in as much as actual deed is. I am not suggesting for one instant that we need 'Thought Police' to root out damaging daydreams which are harmful to the rest of the cosmos! However, I will put forward that those thoughts which we dwell on or infuse with a great deal of imagination and life are those which can take on their own astral shape and form and will be an affecting energy in themselves. Hence the little black cloud feeling when one is with a person suffering from depression.

These thought energies can take of a serious dimension of their own. Worry or fear are two particularly bad ones to dwell upon constantly. I have shaken hands with someone who had been quite down and concerned about their life and they left me with a large shapeless black form. I made that physical connection to them and like a wire they passed their thought energies to me. As a psychic I could manifestly see this as a large entity made of anxiety. The person walked away feeling better whilst I dealt with the 'black mass' that they had created for themselves by constantly brooding on a certain topic. Even non-psychic people could feel the presence of this energy which was then swiftly dismantled. It was not a ghost, spirit or any human creature. It was an energy-entity filled with angst. It could be blown apart and scattered by someone who was aware of what they were seeing. To anyone else it would have left a nasty, dreary draining energy in their house. Such entities have no intelligence but feed directly from the energy that made them, lest they shrink away. Therefore they inspire worry or fear in order to stay fat. Hence by this example that even our thoughts can affect others. Nothing we do is in isolation.

We can transfer this 'connectedness' across to our relationship with the environment and its inhabitants (the two legged and the four legged, the feathered and the finned, the stone people...the Native American terminology seems appropriate to describe our natural kin on this planet). Everything contains that life spark energy and nothing is better or lesser. Therefore what right have we to claim dominion over the birds and beasts? They have their own life force energy for their own soul species as we do. We cannot incarnate as a tiger as we have a human type soul. This does not make the tiger inferior, only different, in the same way as other human soul kinds are not inferior but different. If we see past the disguises such as a tiger body or a Chinese body or a snake body or a business man body or whatever shell we wear in the manifest then we are dealing once again with pure and raw soul energy. Soul energy needs love, respect and understanding. It doesn't need controlling, repressing, abusing or dismissing. The lesson here is that we are linked again as a natural element of energy to the other energies unlike our own. With this view point, we can only feel a gentle curiosity and interest in the differences as opposed to a superior and crushing disregard for them. We are all part of the same source.

The whole process of incarnation seems a difficult and fraught one with all these lessons! How much easier it is to go bulldozing through life with a single-minded purpose! How much simpler to think that animals are less intelligent than us and therefore cant feel pain in the same way. How much more satisfying only to worry about ones own family/house/car and to claim that the rest isn't your fault, that it is nothing to do with you! How much more enjoyable to boo and hiss the enemy and to insult the side you don't support! It all seems far too complicated being connected to everything. And besides, who wants to do this all over again anyway? What is the point?!

From that perspective, not a great deal! From a renewed and positive perspective in which there are possibilities and probabilities then there is a whole fresh lease of life. For everything we do or learn, we are not alone! When things are hard we can know, and truly believe, that they have been hard before and that the soul will survive the grief or pain. The view of seeing the eternal soul with its many and varied forays into incarnation, accompanied by other souls who are of the same type, is one which can open us to really being human avatars of the principles of spirit.... kindness, compassion and personal understanding.

Judy Hall, the excellent and respected past-life astrologer discusses the whole question of soul group/type in her book *Hands Across Time* (Findhorn, 1997) which adds to the reasoning of why we bother to incarnate. To use her words a pool of spiritual essence contains the whole (referring to the root energy or Greater Spirit). She goes on to state that a piece of this breaks off the soul group and then continues to subdivide into individual souls. She sees the purpose of this as the parts can come together again to unite and reunite, sharing all that has been learned. She sees the feeling of familiarity which accompanies an incarnate meeting with such kindred souls as the interweaving web of soul connections...each part of the web will feel like a soul mate, some more strongly than others depending on how far from the original branching the souls have moved and on the experiences that they have had together in former lives.

From this, she draws the purpose of incarnation to be change and growth, the kindred soul offering a familiar guiding presence with which to learn acceptance and our own inner rightness (as opposed to a universal and dictatorial form of judged correctness). In *Deja Who?* (Findhorn, 1998) Ms. Hall concludes that this aspect of the soul being part of something bigger, with more than its own existence at stake, is that we are lead to generously share from our hearts all that we have learned so that humanity evolves. With this sense of collective responsibility and sharing as the nub of existing in the material plane comes a feeling of being part of a huge bolt of energy (rather than being some piddling little nothing who sees no point to her/his dreary life!) If we can open up to this idea of being part of a vast team which is, in turn, part of a huge collective, then the sense of fighting through life alone is removed.

Incarnate life is not meant to be a fight but just an experience! When we can believe in the possibility that we are soul-energy, housed temporarily in a chosen form then we can begin to relax a little. Of course things matter, things from the mundane to the life changing. Of course we are not meant to realise our eternal nature and then spend the rest of this life sleeping and pondering our navels, knowing we will get another crack of this life-game again sometime! We are meant to care and be motivated by incarnate life, we are supposed to feel passionately about things on this level, temporary as they may be. We elect, in pure soul-mode, to incarnate to have our soul imprinted with these resonant feelings, negative or positive. What is most appropriate for us this time around may be harsh or unjust in human terms. Yet it is more beneficial to acknowledge that possibility that this really is just a learning experience in the school of life. Also that life is a many levelled process, not just this linear and ordered progression that the human self experiences here. More on this later.

There are two points that we should look at here, the first being that of soul learning patterns and the second being that of karmic implications and karma itself. The former is best seen from the perspective of the overview, something which can be obtained from a dialogue with either the higher self or the Spirit Guide. The latter comes from this overview by means of an assessment of our choices within these patterns. Karma is a much used term which can be used to cover, quite literally, a multitude of sins. These can range from well, I stole his girlfriend so no doubt someone will steal mine this time (leading to a laissez-faire attitude to the girlfriend in questioning the fatalistic belief that she will be going off with someone else anyway) to he broke my bicycle when I was a child so his karma was to break his leg last week. He was always a nasty person. Karma is not such a black and white system of cause and effect, like all universal principles it can be active over centuries in a subtle, yet effective, manner. As Mark Ryan and Chesca Potter state in their *Greenwood Tarot* handbook, the universe has a long memory.

It is this cosmic memory and the nature of universal patterns that we shall come to first. As was often quoted in the HTV children's series *Robin of Sherwood* (a Pagan-orientated adaptation of the symbolism of the legend) nothing is ever forgotten. The thing that is never forgotten in this instance is referring to the bigger patterns, choices and decisions that we make whilst incarnate. It is not referring to the fact that the universe will remember the fact that when you were seven you once tripped up a boy at school! It does not refer to the fact that if you took someone's sandwich once when you were at school you are destined to have something important of yours stolen in your next earthly incarnation! It refers to larger events and patterns which affect our lives and so those of other people, to positive or negative effect.

In the most extreme cases on either side of this, a self sacrifice for a loved one would be ultimately something to be rewarded in later years/lifetimes...the reward may not be directly related but would be reaped in a 'what goes around, comes around' sense. The energy we put out into the cosmos gets translated into a new pattern, adapted accordingly. The murder of an enemy would be a scenario which needed to be explored in order for the lesson to be derived from this travesty of human error. Both these actions affect your own soul and those of other folk, outwards and onwards in a ripple effect, therefore the universe stores the vibration of these memories. They are started upon cosmic energy files which can be replayed at any time, rather like a house releasing the vibration of events which occurred within its walls (providing a haunting in effect). It is an emotional charge. This is what is never forgotten. The energies involved are the key.

It is these stored vibrations which shape the patterns and lessons of our incarnations. The mundane, the day to day grind of being alive (sleeping, preparing food, washing clothes etc.) does not feature in many past life recall sessions and it does not have a lot of affect on other lives we may have. Like the physical shell it is but a transient part of being a manifest being. Unless, of course, one has a passion for washing or cooking or sleeping!) Passion is a strong enough feeling to be carried over as a soul memory. Passion is rarely forgotten and often repeated across incarnations, especially the star-crossed and ill-fated kind! Any feeling of injustice is a passionate one, one that grips the soul in a cycle of needing to incarnate in order to put things in order. Of course, one souls idea of order is another persons lesson, no soul-need can be fulfilled in isolation, of course.

If we make a large enough etheric imprint (a hand-print on the fabric of existence, as it were) then we are destined to feel this energy over and again until we are in harmony with it, until it is resolved, learned, sorted. In the case of the vibration of love, devotion and selfless giving then the return to experience this would be strong. Once someone has experienced this they can feel more equipped to pass it on into the chain of existence. With the anger, fear and disturbance set of emotions then there may be opportunities to be on the receiving end of these powerful feelings. Such experiences give us renewed perspectives from other angles. If we had just one life in one body we would never gain that rounded edge and that compassion that such old souls have achieved. By walking in many shoes and by the giving and receiving of strong emotional charges we as souls can progress and give back to others who are connected to us.

With these patterns we see the difference between the mistake itself and the lesson that comes from it. It is only the lesson, or the lack of learning, that resonates for the soul. The mistake itself is another transient piece of human detritus. It is the kind of mistake that it was which counts towards the lesson, not the costume, set and staging of the mistake itself. Children are prone to making rash judgements and mistakes, as are adults. If the childish 'sandwich stealer' that I made an example of earlier continues to steal, oblivious to the discomfort it causes to the owner, or indeed, because of the discomfort, then surely the thief needs to understand what they are doing. However, if this one mistake is all it is and the thief feels guilt then the lesson is valid and the repercussions unnecessary. Even if the thief steals again and then feels that they would not like this happening to them, and so stops thieving, then the lesson is certainly learned. It is always 'I would not like this to happen to me, therefore I will not do it to them' that makes the best lesson. This comes from direct experience.

The overview of incarnate patterns, patterns such as lives of crime, lives of martyrdom, lives of disablement or lives of greed, can give us a clearer idea of why we seem to run around in circles in this life. If we give credence to the a concept of many lives, many selves, then we can be shown far-memories and we can put together a bigger picture of our souls dilemmas and doings on earth. We may do this via the tools of mediation or trance work. Both may be actively participated in by you the individual. You need no third party to interpret who you were, or indeed, who you are. For you are who you are because of who you were, as regards your past in this life and in other lives. You may access the overview for yourself with either of these two tried and tested techniques.

Note: All such work should be done with a sincere heart and a good and focused intention. It is imperative to have a clear objective in mind before wishing to obtain a bigger picture on your soul-patterns and learning. A question such as "Why do I seem to always end up in the same sort of destructive relationship?" Or "Why do I feel such an aversion to childbearing but meet men who would like children?" Or "Why can I not find success in this line of work when I tried so hard to get here?" would be appropriate. There will, no doubt, be a past-life link in these cases.

Remember, you are looking at your soul patterns. You are not looking to place blame or appoint responsibility to anyone but yourself. You may recognise familiar souls with you in the dance of incarnation. Yet it is vital to realise that it is your learning and your patterns which are your business to find out about. You can do nothing about the patterns of another kindred soul, although you may well see how you fit together on that level. This work is between you and your self/soul and should be taken seriously without a day-tripping attitude to checking out past/other lives. You may be shown symbols, rather than actual life material. Record all that you see, however sketchy, on paper directly afterwards. Have a glass of water and a biscuit handy for this period after the session. It will help to ground you in incarnate/ manifest reality....as this is were you have chosen to dwell, for now, and remaining half in the Other Realms is not beneficial to your whole person.

The Meditation or Trancework Path

Objective: To obtain an overview of the important patterns within your incarnations. (N.B. This can be with regard to any specific problem which you have in mind.)

1. Firstly find a quiet and restful place with no distractions. Settle yourself comfortably in a way which suits your body type and needs. There is no universally correct way to meditate in terms of position. You may meditate on the toilet if it is a quite enough place! (or maybe the only place that you wont be disturbed in!) The bath is an excellent place to meditate, water being most conducive to 'seeing'. Please do not force yourself to sit cross-legged because it supposedly looks appropriate!

2. Relax in any way that you find pleasing as regards aids to creating an ambience. Count your breathing

until it becomes slow and deep. Let the stomach expand comfortably as you breathe in and then contract as you exhale slowly. Feel the breath as a wave, a release, washing through your body. Breathe in incense or have a quiet instrumental tape playing in the background (be aware that tapes have a nasty habit of clicking off after thirty or so minutes. This can be distracting!) Take your time and let your mind be as empty as you can, with any extraneous thoughts being allowed to float off, acknowledged but unattended to. I often find it useful to imagine a host of voices of all different types and volumes chattering at once. I let them talk, at first I hear the odd line of gossip and then I gradually tune them out, as if I were daydreaming at a particularly dull party. I enjoy the sensation of restful nothingness and appreciate the time I have given myself to drift.

3. Do not fret if you fall asleep at this point! It often happens to begin with, do not be harsh with your self but try to approach this activity with a little energy in the future! It is important and should be given a bit of quality time, not two minutes before bed!

4. Now you must imagine a protective shell or cloak or coating around yourself, both physically and mentally. Some suggestions for appropriate protections are a suit of armour which is silver tinged with a luminous blue glow, (a super-natural suit!) which covers the person entirely from head to foot and is complete with a helmet which allows for vision and speech. Do not imagine this suit to be heavy but of a lightweight and flexible substance, perhaps an extra-terrestrial metal which cannot be penetrated but which has great flexibility. The criteria for protection is that the astral traveller (i.e. you) should be clad from head to toe in a close fitting silver and blue garb. This can be a blue

neoprene surfers outfit complete with a sci-fi style head mask with silver accessories or it could be a skin-tight latex cat-suit with a full face cover. As long as it covers the criteria then there are no limits to what your imagination can conjure up for you!

There can be silver symbols/mirrored panels/ reflective shiny inserts at the crucial psychic centres or portals of the body. These are especially welcomed at the third/minds eye, throat and heart areas. the solar plexus, lower back and sexual centre may also need an extra bit of protection. The blue or the gold of the suit itself is a protective energy and the silver is a reflective one....all unwanted accessing of your psychic centres will be reflected back at the sender.

Try not to change this protective garb too often in your meditative lead-up. Familiarity with the garb brings a feeling of safety and routine which makes it less likely that you will forget to do this step. By all means add to the original, better it, but try not to chop and change concepts. No astral work should ever be continued without this step. It is important and should never be forgotten. I am not trying to worry the reader but to instill something as important as looking across the road before we step into it. The astral/Otherworld of trance and meditation is not safe. It need not be dangerous but it can be full of shape-shifting, deception and unexpected events. Be protected and you will be on guard and will have taken sensible measures. Once your protective clothing, feel the earth beneath your feet and your earthly connection to it.

5. Now imagine, see in the third eye, minds eye or psychic centre of self a place of great peace, beauty and safety. This is your own personal safe place which will be the setting for encounters with your spirit mentor or Guide. It is here that you may wish to meet with other souls, including parts of your own eternal energy spark

(some of which is not incarnate right now, perhaps). You may wish to gain insights from yourself in past or other life modes. You may wish to speak with the souls of others in your lives. You may wish to speak with the souls of those who have passed on from these earthly levels in order to get guidance and reassurance for their relatives. For now, however, we will concern ourselves with creating this minds-eye space for the purpose of attaining information about our own life patterns.

There are no limits to what the minds-eye can dream up and so I can leave it to you where your idea of a tranquil and idyllic setting would be. Remember two vital things. Firstly, this is your space and it goes by your rules. You are essentially the architect, artist and creator of whatever you chose to see and this cannot be altered by another. Secondly, once you regularly start to visit your space then you will add power to it. the more you see it, the more it will become an astral reality and actually exist in the Otherworlds. As with the thought-form creations we mentioned earlier, we can literally create our own super-reality which is just as valid as the one which we perceive here in the now. Vision and psychic focus can bring a real sense of life to the place you choose to picture.

For balance, I suggest that there should be representatives of the four elements in your safe place, water (how different a setting could be by just changing the nature of the water in it...from turbulent crashing ocean to majestic tumbling waterfall to still lake) fire (the sun, a bonfire, volcano,) earth (hills, standing stones, mountains, fields, trees, a beach) and the effect of air upon the landscape, (corn swaying in the breeze, wind whipping autumn hued leaves around your feet). The lists are endless, the myriad of permutations is inexhaustible. I will give one example for those who may find this hard to see initially. there is no harm in using this example, it will work perfectly well in your minds-eye, but do try and embellish it with your personal preferences (a tall, oak tree rather than a tree, etc.).

Example: You walk through a field with the sun on your back, admiring the wild flowers and following the track left by a wild animal. The track takes you to a woodland setting with a lush verdant feel of midsummer to it. In order to reach a clearing you have to pass through the middle of a hollow tree which had formed a natural passage way. It is quite imperative that you create either an archway, doorway or tunnel into another level of your environment...you could pass between two rocks, under overhanging trees, through a rose covered wicker arch, under a bridge, down a candlelit passage to a cave etc.

This symbolic 'passing through' means that you are able to perceive a deeper level of travel into this, your realm. You can now hear water and a stream runs across your path. You cross it using three stepping stones. Before you in the clearing is a raised grassy knoll with a tree-stump on it. You chose to sit there, to listen to the water babbling by, the birds singing and the warm wind lifting the leaves.

Creating the safe place is a simple as that. It is the effort of adding detail and feeling your presence within the landscape which take patience and discipline. This isn't a game, as I have already stated. It is an art and a science, a job of work and a focus of effort. As with everything else in life, the more you put in (in terms of colour, sound, personalised information etc.) the more you will receive (in terms of visual clarity and communication). If you make a real living place then you have far better chances of encountering a real energised living soul there. You have made a half-way place for them to meet you. They cannot come into the world as souls without an enormous amount of effort in order to be seen by our manifest dense selves.

We cannot go into the Otherworld proper as we are corporeal beings and can only travel soul-wise into a space such as this. We are not readily capable of comprehending the Otherworld when we are still housed in bodily form. Otherworldly and discarnate energy is something only a purely disembodied (between lives) soul can understand. It is a question of levels of existence.

(N.B. It is valid to add here that it is more beneficial to create an outdoor environment as a safe space as it needs the elements to be present and not just a suggestion outside of a window. Try to avoid seeing houses in this context. However, houses come in very handy when we do an exercise to access other lives directly).

> 6. When you have created this place (and you may wish to do this routine half a dozen times before you feel ready for this next stage as unless you are a highly visual or imaginative person in an active sense then this will take time to become real for you) find somewhere to sit within it. Sit and enjoy the place for a few moments and begin to feel a part of it all, as we are with all nature, this being a natural environment. Use smell and touch as well as sight and sound. Become 'in place'. Then imagine you are holding a tool. This can be a knife or sword, wand or stick, staff, arrow or any other a manner of item which has sacred connotations and can be used as a pointer. It could be that you wish to use a finger for this job if you feel uncomfortable holding something else.

Imagine pure blue firelight coming from the tip of this finger or tool. Draw this fire in a circle around yourself where you sit, until you are sat in a small circle of blue flame. Then, a metre or two away from you in your direct line of sight, inscribe another circle on the ground. Make it big enough for another person to stand up in. Then stand up within your own circle and using your pointer direct your blue energy at the other circle. Ask something like "Great Spirit, I ask that you send to me my true Guide, my only mentor, that spirit which is here to help my own. Let them be revealed within this circle".

At this point do not be afraid and try not to force things, simply wait. Someone will come, as you have a Guide and this is their role. If you are aware of a presence, a glow or a partially visible being then greet them and direct this energy from the pointer at them (some people use a mirror for this task, this is a personal choice and one best decided on by experiencing both tools). Ask something like "Are you my one true Guide? May your actual identity be revealed to me now." At this point the being who has appeared may do many things. If they genuinely are who they calm to be then they may glow brighter, materialise more fully or grow in size. If they are not then they will either disappear or change drastically into what they really are. If this is the case then keep approaching Spirit until the Guide comes through. The astral is full of jokers and time wasters who will pretend to be just about anything for some attention! Be patient, do not rush, simply hold out for your true mentor to appear.

When they do appear then do not be surprised how they look. Your soul type will determine who is most appealing to you, be this by past life links or archetypal energies. Some souls bond easiest with representatives of a Celtic energy, in full Celtic regalia whilst others have affinities with strictly Norse appearances. Some souls have Nuns or Native Americans or people from the lost city of Atlantis...it depends entirely on your own soul group and resonance within it. The face may be familiar with you from this life or another... the Guide may be a relative or long lost friend. In this case, they are wearing a guise that you recognise on an earth level (as you are currently earth bound) but they are no longer only that character. They are soul. As are the Guides who come through in 'fancy dress' as Tibetan monks, Samurai warriors or Chinese doctors. Guides either work on the recognition or the resonant principle. Either way, it matters little, other than you may feel a link to their appearance in some shape or form, one with which you may feel comfortable. Guides are there to help, after all. So do not be surprised at what you see. And if you see nothing but feel or hear things then this too is valid. Not everyone is a 'visual' person.

> 7. Now that contact is established, you the quester can ask any number of things. However, to start with you could ask the Guide to give you an overview of this incarnation and its patterns. Do not expect this to be a prediction of the future. The future is a tangled web of possibility and probability. The Guides see more than us but they cannot determine absolute outcome. They can only suggest the best course to take and allow for the free will, of ourselves and others to alter the main frame. We are free to go as we please within this broad structure but the Guide can wisely advise on the most appropriate paths to take for your own souls learning. You could ask something like "what are the specific lessons that my soul has chosen in this incarnation?" or "what are the main tasks that I have set myself in this lifetime?" or "what are the patterns that need to be attended to by the person I am today?"

You may receive Guidance by way of direct speech, imagery and symbolism, feelings and memories within you coming to the surface (far-memory of all our souls past catalogue of experience, stored deep within us and only accessible in the now when there is a purpose to remembering. Life in the now would be useless under a constant barrage of such memory) or by way of a 'cinematic experience'. Sometimes the Guide will have the ability to project your key moments which shape the patterns before you as if you were viewing a film. The Guide will chose the best method to get information across powerfully but succinctly at that time. Do not expect to have no interaction with them, there will be a sense of feeling attached to what you see/feel/recall. This is your soul's truth. Do not fear as the guide is your most constant ally and is there to support you through any pain or lingering regret. They can also help you to understand tragedy or negative patterns within incarnation that you alone cannot see any sense in. Such is the beauty of this Guide/soul dialogue! And joy of joys, we all have a Guide! This is not an exclusive club but a right to which we can all have access.

8. Do not outstay your welcome here although it can be tempting! If your special place is more alluring than the now then maybe you can address why this is the case? Learn things in chunks and go back to 'the now'. An information overload will not be easily remembered back in the now level and so the trip will be a waste of time if you hear too much but cannot retain the knowledge. Seeing as yourself and the Guide stay firmly within your blue flame circles (at least until you establish a working relationship in your safe space and then you can dispense with the circles and just use the 'pointing' technique) all you need to do is to thank the Guide for the time, love and effort and ask that they now go back to that place in the universe where they are meant to be at this time. This applies to all guest visitors to your space. Courtesy is a great asset as well as vigilance to intruding energies. Be alert and be confident in your powers there. Be polite, even to unpleasant guests (you will get them eventually, not all astral forms are aesthetically or intellectually pleasing!)

9. When you have said a goodbye, with thanks, you may leave your own blue circle and retrace your footsteps until you come back to the place where you entered your realm. Stay at that place, feeling the

sensation of being in the now returning ...hear the ticking clock, feel the carpet or armchair, smell your own scent. Slowly regain your vision of the room and sit up or stand up gradually. Move your fingers and toes.

Note your memories and findings down immediately after drinking and eating a little. You have now got access to the Otherworld, one of the biggest privileges one can have as an incarnate human soul. Use it wisely, often and with focused purpose. Remember that guidance is just that...it is not having a fortune teller on tap. It is having access to someone whose overview is broader than yours and who can advise accordingly.

Using the direct method, the channelled pathway to information.

Objective: To ask a focused question about the nature of incarnation or specific areas of your own life patterns.

You should be in a comfortable position with a pen held loosely in your operative writing hand and plenty of blank paper (plus something to lean on). When you become confident at this technique you may switch the pen to the inactive hand, the one which feels unfamiliar, and let the direct messages come through in a way which you as a human being can interfere with less. The operative hand tends to be used in a more restrained and intellectual way, the inactive being more instinctive and spontaneous.

Have something to eat and drink on hand for after the proceedings. Grounding after the event is as important as protection. If either are left undone or incomplete then the practitioner of these techniques will feel vulnerable, confused and any number of other variables associated with unwanted astral intervention. These can be as commonplace as dizziness or headache to a full-blown Poltergeist-style haunting by energies that have become attached to the quester.

Follow steps one to four as described in the Trancework path. Then -

5. Write with intent and focus the nature of the communication that you wish to channel from the energies of the universe. If you are aware of your Guide, address it to them personally. If not, you can still aim it at them and they will hear you. Alternatively, an address to another part of the self (usually known as the 'higher self', although height and depth, black and white have no literal meaning here. Higher in this case means more connected to the astral levels than our manifest selves. This 'height' will lead to the self having more of the detached overview of this incarnation, in a similar way to the Guide's way of working. This part of the self may actually not be incarnation right now, but in attendance none the less. Ask a specific question about the nature of life's patterns. Do say something as tight as "where does my fear of flying come from and how may I break the pattern?" If the question is not limiting then the nature of the communication will change from a targeted answer to a rambling diatribe on the nature of existence. As fascinating as this may be, it is hard to stem the flow of such a spirit driven piece of prose (spirit has little opportunity to express itself manifestly and rejoices in it but often loses sight of our time limited world! Also of the exhaustion that may arise from channelling pages of esoteric thought!) Do try and focus on a single issue at a time.

6. With your eyes closed or open (if they are shut, ensure the paper is readily to hand) hold the pen

loosely in either hand and allow it to move by itself. This may happen literally without any awareness of the words that are written or there may be a guiding voice inside the head which instructs what should be written. Either way, there should be a sense of the message being passed through you, the spirit using you only as a means to make their words manifest...you become a wire, conducting specific energy between this world and the other. If there is any intervention from your manifest persona (hesitation, rationalising what is written, putting it into your own words etc.) then the flow is stemmed and communication will become patchy. The idea is that it is a flow, not a dialogue between two parties. For this to work effectively then you must become an extension of the pen, an instrument only.

7. The channelled writing should be concluded by a thanks and an invitation to participate again, if appropriate, should be made. This act of spiritual transference should be finished by a grounding using the eating and drinking ritual to earth the soul back into the body (it will have become partially disconnected when this channelling happened, part of the soul going into the astral realms allowing the spirit guidance to come through unhindered. This does not mean you are out of control, but relaxed and not in a manifest mode of intervention. This is where protection comes in, if one is adequately protected then there is no need to worry.)

The written guidance may have poured out faster than you could think or make connections between hand and eye so that some of the guidance is bound to be illegible. With practice, one need not interfere with the natural flow of information coming through, but it is possible to modify its speed and control. In fact, if one uses this technique regularly then the nature of the correspondent in terms of style and presentation become more familiar, even as a sort of code. As with all spirit guidance, for example through a ouija board where the pointer may spell out words and phrases quicker than the participants can read them, they are operating in their time, not ours. Their speed of delivery can be politely tempered and attuned to your personal abilities so do not feel disheartened if your first attempts are nought but scribble!

This manner of gaining an overview on the matters of incarnate life and the patterns thereof is well worth persevering with as it gives such direct results. The meditation technique can be visually more spectacular and entertaining but within its framework one must always make allowances for forgetting what we see/are told and interpreting the imagery incorrectly. Yet with the trance technique of journeying in meditation there is far more of a feel of the situation than with guided writing, so each mode has its positive and negative side. I recommend a blend of both methods, as and when required. Always with a serious attitude and not a need for strange entertainment.

Spirit usually has a humourous way of dealing with those who dabble thus! This way runs the gamut from moving someone's keys around (a frustrating thing if ever there was one!) to strange smells and unexplained noises. Hiding keys that you just know that you left somewhere can be a great waste of time...not harmful but personally annoying!

Spirit also tends to move household items and leave them in unlikely places...you really do know that you have been got by Spirit when it leaves the toilet roll on top of a lightshade! Messing about or dabbling with spiritual energies can be dangerous in the extreme, especially if there is no protection or correct departure procedure used. Generally though, it is well meant but unfocussed playing with it that ensures an equally gentle and well meaning warning from the other side!

In conclusion to this chapter on learning and the purpose and nature of incarnation I will use a quote from Rae Beth, Witch Priestess and a personal friend of mine with whom I have shared other lives. In her book *Reincarnation and the Dark Goddess* (Hale, 1994) she uses a piece of channelled vision to illustrate the point of incarnate life. "I heard a voice say that in that first ocean, our own perfect potential was to be found- the being we could become at our finest and best, the Mothers original dream for our strength and happiness". She goes on to express this as an essence, a compacted image, a possibility. A dream of life. Using the concepts and techniques discussed and shared in this chapter, you too may access such wisdoms and make your own poetry concerning the dance of incarnation.

You may wish to acknowledge, and give thanks for, your own unique blend of energies which can be expressed in so many ways using so many guises and settings. In the next chapter we look at these masks that the soul can wear, why it may choose them and what relevance these other selves have to the now.

Poppy Palin 99

Chapter Three

Mask Making...
The Role of the Soul
Vehicle

The soul that we have is capable of growing and becoming improved, hurt, scarred or developed. It can experience damage or it can experience nurture. Yet it cannot change what it is fundamentally. It cannot break from its type and essential nature. It can be an adaptation of what it is, at core, but it cannot go against its grain in entirety. It is as it is. It is only very unexpected or shocking bodily injury, injustice, torment or forced removal from loved ones which can actually damage the soul beyond the body. These wounds are they which drive the soul-self on and on to find these other souls to replay these scenes in different guises until the terrible mistakes of past incarnations can be put right, forgiven and healed.

The soul does not carry all scars from all lives. It is only the huge and spirit breaking acts...the massacre of a village or destruction of a people, acts of indignity such as gang rape or torture, being falsely accused and brutally killed for something you did not do...these are the things which mar the soul. But they do not change it. Once in manifest, incarnate, bodily form the soul may seek to meet the other souls in the past scenario in order for justice to be done and a replay occur (obviously a symbolic one, not a full scale war). It is only the manifest personality that may act thoughtlessly and destructively in retaliation. The soul has a hand in the personality but it is different to it. The personality is transient and affected by the body and circumstances that it is in. The personality is based on the soul type but it is only human and it can change. Soul type contributes to personality but ultimately they are different, separate. The personality is not a permanent/constant as is the soul, but it does reflect some of the souls inherent qualities.

The soul may have various root or core characteristics, despite any scars it may have attained during bodily life. These are deep traits which can, as has been previously stated, be developed or improved. Such core attributes could be;

a) Self-motivated.

b) Creative.

c) Observant.

d) Easily bored.

e) Self-sufficient.

f) Rebellious.

g) Psychic and sensitive, daydreamer.

h) Communicator.

These are basic and fundamental attributes of a soul-type. They could be embellished by a personality like this;

a) Runs their own business, cannot work for a boss.

b) Creates hand painted pottery in their own studio.

c) Some of the painted edging and decoration is extremely fiddly.

d) Gets frustrated doing the cleaning up and accounts afterwards.

e) Can only have their partner in the studio when they feel like it. Cannot live with their partner, likes own space too much but loves the partner anyway.

f) Gets annoyed when shops will not take the work and feels personally affronted. Wants to know why.

g) Can drift off in the afternoons if they do not keep focused. Tends to imagine the future a lot. Can often read peoples thoughts and intentions so tries not to get too close to them

h) Is able to teach pottery at an adult class once a week.

So, we can see the development of soul attributes into incarnate personality. It is only when incarnate circumstance intervenes that the personality gets thrown off line as to the souls needs or intentions. For example, using the previous lists;

a) In the current economic climate such a business cannot survive without compromise.

b) Mass produced items are what the consumer desires and there are not enough customers for exquisite one-off pieces.

c) With such pressures upon them they cannot concentrate on the detailed work without worrying that nobody will wish to buy it anyway.

d) Starts feeling as if there is no point keeping things in order as they are going to fail anyway.

e) Withdraws from their partner because they are too involved with their own worries. Becomes moody, irritable and distant.

f) Gets annoyed with the general ethos of society which does not support truly innovative or creative people.

g) Gets depressed and nervous as they are sure that the world is a bad place with things conspiring against them personally. Gets upset at all the negative things happening in the world generally.

h) Because they feel that they will be pushed into doing another unsuitable job in order to make enough money they feel frustrated, run down and more depressed. This leads to one minor illness after another and they are unable to attend or give their college class very often. So they feel more guilty about letting people down, but then also think what is the point in teaching them pottery anyway, they'll never get a job from it.

It is clear to see how these external factors may influence the incarnation and affect the persona the soul has taken on. As these are not life-threatening or dreadful events in themselves, they will not harm the soul. However, the souls natural way of being will affect how the personality deals with the life-crises as it sees them to be. Also, any deep trauma or shaping that the soul may have taken on in other lives will affect how the persona reacts to circumstance. These soul scars may show up as feelings of persecution magnified (in our example, the character we are discussing feels victimised by the world in general as they are not able to follow their career of choice) or as concerns over other individuals (who they may have encountered before in other lives) or as a fear of repeating a pattern that they facing on some subconscious, hidden level.

It can be observed that such irrational experiences can be traced directly back to the events which made the soul scar in the first place. The general feel of the current dilemma or anxiety, if it shows no root cause in the now, will be a reflection of the initial trauma. The person who feels persecuted at the slightest hint of adversity has experienced persecution...maybe as a Jew, an occultist, an early Christian or whatever. The person who cannot breathe and begins to hyper-ventilate when near a swimming pool has had a bad drowning experience. The person who experiences a nameless paranoia whenever a certain person enters their life is recovering from being betrayed by them in another time. The manifest guise or clothes that an original problem wore are not vitally important. What matters is the vibration the shock wave caused...a vibration of persecution or paranoia or suffocation. In chapter four we will cover the nature of dealing directly with such remnant fears and links of other lives.

These other-life vibrations, or soul lesions, may make the person experience seemingly irrational worries, jealousies or desires. These may over ride any sense of logic that they may feel about their circumstances. Such feelings are usually associated with the individual having opted to re-enact these patterns and scenarios again in life in order to put things to rights or to lay them to rest. This agreement of the soul is made pre-birth and usually concerns the soul involved having to make amends. The soul agrees to a set of circumstances which may seem hard, uncomfortable or downright painful to the manifest personality. The soul, however, knows what to expect and finds the reserves of energy and patience needed for the manifest persona to be able to cope with trying situations.

Such situations can also be initiated by other souls who have agreed to put their own side of things right. You as a soul may have had no active part in agreeing to this and so it will come as a surprise, even on a soul level, to find yourself in a difficult scenario with someone familiar who seeks to sort out a past pattern. These influences, felt on a deep level, will be the ones that the persona finds the most difficult to cope with manifestly. When the soul has made its own agreements to meet other souls again or to try something out again then the persona finds it hard but has the souls resolve and purpose to spur it on. With an unexpected soul reunion or piece of soul drama then the soul itself is more open to mystification and astonishment and cannot give the persona the back up it requires.

This makes the clear difference between soul learning and the persona. The soul can learn from the tiniest nuance to a full scale and unexpected confrontation. The persona may seem to be floundering, unhappy or in a state of stagnation whilst the soul is busy gathering information and lessons. The delineation between soul and personality may seem unkind but its truth is that the body/persona is nothing more than the soul's puppet. The body is, after all, cast aside as if it were a rag doll at the end of life. It is chosen in a pre-birth agreement and will fit the soul's needs. Therefore, the nature of the parents, their location and status and their gene pool to be utilised are all considered. Any impairments likely as a result of their union will also be taken into account by the soul. Maybe even chosen specifically because of such impairments. The soul may need the learning experience of being trapped inside a body which functions inadequately, or with a brain which does not respond to its wishes, or maybe without actual sight or hearing. All such things are considered and so the actual body that the soul chooses is important. Important but not permanent. In its most basic terms, it is a soul-garment, a suit of clothes chosen to fit that life's specifications.

This is not to say that being incarnate isn't a process which is sacred in itself. It is not suggesting that incarnate or earthly existence is throw-away and that we should have no respect for our bodily shells or that of others. Moreover, it is not suggesting that we have no respect for the earth itself. Without the wonderful gifts of incarnate/manifest being then we should never experience the physical side of existence at all. The profound pleasure and pain that comes from this mode of dwelling in flesh is that which lingers longest in the spirit. The joy of nature, of our bodies, of being in different guises and different places is not one to be thought of as disposable in a blasé or rude way. Flesh is certainly disposable, not eternal. This is a truth. However, there is a intense respect due to the earth and to manifest beings as they are our hosts. We are, as soul, the guests. We should leave the hosts domain in order for the next set of visitors.

Going back to our example of the soul (whose basic type, adopted persona and the effect of circumstance upon it have been discussed), let us now consider what suitable guises or roles it may have been most suited to be born into through time. Broadly speaking, there would be two ways that this soul could learn. Firstly by wearing personalities or bodies which harmonised entirely with the natural mode of the soul. Given its basic attributes these sort of appropriate incarnations would be;

a) A monastic scribe.

b) An Egyptian hieroglyph painter or sacred artist.

c) A Celtic Craftsman.

d) An Oracle in Ancient Greece.

e) A Druid Priest.

f) A preacher or disciple of Gnostic gospels.

g) A University lecturer in art history.

h) An embroiderer of Indian costume.

i) A creator of one-off handmade shoes.

j) A wandering minstrel.

Any of these lifestyles or trades would have been appropriate for such a soul...or any of the soul type or group from which it came. Given the slight variation of emphasis of traits within each individual soul in the group, this list could branch off in several directions whilst maintaining its basic theme. Also given the full rounded nature of the soul we are discussing, there would be aspects of any of these lifestyles which would goad as well as stimulate it. For example, the Monks life may make the souls free-spirited rebellious streak come to the fore and they may ask too many questions. The preacher life may be too public without enough privacy and retreat. The stitching of Indian garments may be too monotonous after a while. However, these are rough frameworks of suitable lives for these soul types.

Sometimes a soul must learn from a most unsuitable life, choosing an incarnation which is diametrically opposed to their type. This may be to get a clearer perspective of living in another persons shoes. Or it may be a harsh lesson for condemning or misunderstanding someone in that position in another life. The circumstances of the incarnation will be hard for the soul to cope with. the persona the soul has will wonder why they seem to be constantly doing the wrong thing with a sense of unease. Maybe in such a case, the soul may chose a persona or body or a lower intelligence, as to spare them the constant bother of feeling out of sorts. It is the soul which must get on with the job of learning whilst the body will act the part in order for the learning conditions to be met. Thus the soul may find itself in an incarnation in a very uncomfortable suit of clothes, one which does not fit their nature but which assists in the process of them understanding more fully. It can help to emphasis what the soul is, at core, and act as an statement of what their type actually is. Sooner or later a soul will try to mould itself into another way of being and the process of trying to do this may act as a clear affirmation of what they really are. Learning can be found everywhere!

For the soul in question, we could suggest some opposite incarnations for it which are completely opposed to its core nature;

a) A Sergeant at Arms.

b) A Catholic Inquisitor.

c) Headmistress of a boarding school.

d) A Footballing personality.

e) A bank manager.

f) A member of Parliament.

g) A Roman slave.

h) A Viking warrior.

It must be kept firmly in mind that these characters or masks are only names we give to the personality. The soul lays no claim upon them only in a very temporary sense. Whilst incarnate, our time scale shifts from the infinite to the blinkered view rendered in the present-personal. It is therefore understandable that whilst discarnate, as pure soul, we can view these persona-characters as nothing but transient and temporary shifts in disguise. However, whilst in flesh as we are now, our view of the progression of other selves that we were and will be again is limited. We can generally only deal with one past-life at a time which makes that feeling of connection with the role, rather than the overall soul purpose, more immediate.

We can tend to get bogged down in the trivia of incarnation, believing it to be the most fascinating part. Who we were, our guises and role-playing masks, is indeed fascinating, from a time-tourist point of view. It is also interesting from an analytical pint of view, knowing what sort of persona our soul would choose besides the one we currently have. However, the real beef of the study of other incarnations are the patterns that they make and build up. Not only our own personal learning patterns but the patterns that we make with other souls, their effects on us and our effect outwards into their environment reaching further than we could know. That is, until we start to look and to actually see the bigger picture.

It is to be expected that you would wish to marvel at the hat you wore in seventeen twenty eight! It is understandable that you would wish to gasp at your smelly countenance during an incarnation in a cave in France in the times before written history! And who would not be curious as to exactly how rich one had been in a life in the Russian aristocracy? But then one should let the trappings of life, effectively costume frippery, be consigned to the great cosmic dressing up box. The real fun comes from looking at the webs of life and of lives. Then we see who we really are behind the mask, who we are as pure soul.

The time when we were first discovering past-lives in Western consciousness, through names such as Arnold Bloxham, Arthur Guirdham, Edgar Cayce or through the case of Bridey Murphy, is now gone. The initial aim of such work was to prove reincarnation existed as fact by providing flawless portraits of historical figures. The new discoveries from this initial foray into characterisation can be made by omitting the details. We will look at the need for verification of past-life truths in the next chapter. Here, it is prudent to state that it no longer matters what is the supposed, perceived truth of the matter. It does not matter if two peoples recollections of the same event differ through far-memory. It does not matter if the person recalls a life that six other people have also encountered as their own. It does not even matter if reincarnation is a truth or a pleasant fantasy. What matters is what the patterns of memory (be that false, or not) tell us about who we really are under all of our manifest clutter.

Two frequently asked questions, firstly the question of star signs or astrology. To hear the glib blanket statement oh so-and-so is a Libra so that explains why they are like that is one which makes me very impatient indeed! The body of the person was born under a particular planetary alignment, this is true. The personality of the body involved may indeed be influenced by the heavenly energies of such an alignment.

Yet, we must remember that it is only the personality and not the actual root being (soul) that can be swayed by such influences. Perhaps the soul also negotiates, in the pre-birth agreement, that the most ideal conception should be achieved for the successful harmonisation of soul, personality and astrological details. Perhaps. However, my own personal view, at this time, is that these are human made definitions of what such-and-such alignment in the stars means, therefore they are as fallible as any other man-made form of truth (like the translation of the Bible, or Koran). How can we state with any sense of security that a person is how they are because they are solely influenced by the astrological movements around their birth time? To be flippant, how may a bunch of rocks in space be the cause of someone being greedy, selfish or extravagant? These are the influences of past-life vibration, present life circumstance and soul-traits coming to bear upon the current manifest persona. Certainly, the planets influence us as heavenly bodies - but do they really have man-made attributes

The second point is, how can a person be a nurse one minute and a murderer the next? Doesn't this mean the person was evil all along and should be punished if she is capable of being so foul? Surely this shows that the person was cunning and devious to hide their true nature in a caring profession? By no means! It is a mixture of circumstance in the manifest life (was this person a victim of abuse themselves?) soul-scars (had this person been murdered by the person that they killed in another life?) and personality defects (is this person prone to depression or rage due to the other two influencing factors?) There is never, ever one straight answer like yes, this person is evil. This person is a composite of influence. This person has made pre-birth agreements to learn certain things in life, as have the people he or she encounters. Maybe this murder was the start of a new pattern, provoked by a combination of torments?

In the following model, we can observe how incarnation, personality and circumstance fit in with the needs and patterns of the soul itself. The map or web that these links form shows us once again how we are not alone and how possibility and probability are involved constantly.

Pre-birth Agreements

(of other known souls) (of the key soul) (of other unknown souls)

Secondary (known to primary) X (same soul group as Y)	Primary (Key Soul) Y (same soul group as X)	Peripheral (Known to neither) Z (different soul type or group)
Unknown events conducive to learning including wishes to meet Y	Pre-ordained events Wishes to meet X	Agreed meetings and events for another soul's learning Needs to meet Y
Directed will and energy plus random Energy of Z	Directed will and energy c Random energy coming from Z	Has free will but soul has agreed for the sake of another's growth
Past life patterns and influences with Y Current life energies affected by Z	Past life patterns and influences with X current life energies affected by interaction of X and Z together	Current life influenced strongly by Y who is in turn connected by soul pattern to X

Desired Outcome = Learning, Growth, Resolution, Healing etc

Indirect circumstantial manifest influences

Desired outcome between X and Y influenced by Z

A new dynamic which resolves the previous links and connections and

a) either forges new ones to be learned from and resolved

or

b) clears the pattern and begins a new one

Chapter Four

Are We One Another?

The title of this chapter is the key question. Do we, as souls, have the potential, in possibility, to incarnate as just about anyone? The simple answer is, as long as it suits our learning programme, then yes. We can no more go for a holiday trip into someone else's shoes than we can truly experience exactly how another soul feels. We cannot experience life as Joe Bloggs but only as our interpretation of Joe Bloggs.

It is far better for us as growing spiritual beings to be our own version of a persona, rather than a pale imitation of someone else's interpretation. Imitation is not the sincerest form of flattery, in this case, although admiring traits in another persona and wishing to incorporate those characteristics into our own act is a different matter.

Think of all the attributes that a person, physically speaking, may have. Then group them into desirable and undesirable. You may use your own honest criteria or use the eyes of your society to view these things according to popular taste. If one is honestly going by the average Western viewpoint at this time then the desirable section may look something like this;

Young,

Tall,

Slim,

Healthy,

Good teeth,

Shiny hair,

Toned physique,

Unblemished skin,

Regular features.

The Hollywood version of desirable human attributes is as above. This permeation of a cultural and aesthetic norm into a wider Western world (and beyond) dictates a stereotypical image of the ideal specimen. One could add to the list such extras as long legs, blonde hair, large breasts etc. I find it incredibly sad that I hear people, over and over, referring to themselves as inadequate, whilst championing this perennially young, elongated, pneumatic form. A form that they are far from being able to aspire to. This can, and does, begin equating to this image as being 'good'. One only has to look at Princess Diana to recognise this. If she had never performed a good deed in her life she would still have been seen as virtuous and worthy. She fitted the stereotype perfectly and therefore must have been perfect inside too. Whilst the person who cannot ever become so proportioned or adorned is somehow lazy, unworthy, and therefore probably not quite so pleasant all round. I only had to set up a Tattoo Studio to hear such comments from clients all the time (for example, "oh please don't look at my fat stomach". "I wish I looked like so-and-so, don't you?"). Our concepts of 'good', 'desirable' etc have become confused and damaging to individuals

It is only reasonable then to compile a general list of those attributes of human form which are treated with disdain, disgust or loathing. These could be said to be;

Baldness,

Signs of Ageing,

Body Fat,

Short stature,

Disability,

Irregular features,

Scars or disfigurement,

Inappropriate body hair.

If this is the case, and there have certainly always been physical norms or desired images across the world (take the paintings of Rubens, for an example, or the Chinese tradition of foot-binding, or the Elizabethan desire to have whiter-than-white skin) then who would wish to incarnate into such an environment unless they were utterly flawless? Surely anyone else who incarnated into a shoddy, badly formed, sickly or puny body would be at a disadvantage immediately? Exactly!

The disadvantage means that one is forced to develop the soul in order for the inner qualities to shine through. The greater the deviation from societies physical norm, the more the soul will have to work at being respected, loved and appreciated. There are lessons to be had in choosing a disadvantaged flesh vehicle. One of them could be that we always need someone who will challenge the norm and push its boundaries by showing that beauty is not just skin deep, no matter how huge or compelling the marketing push to the contrary is.

Following this logic, would it be fair to say that not only are there physical characteristics that are more preferable than others, but also manifest circumstances. Here are two examples of a body and situation that a soul may be born into;

Black female illegitimate child

Born in Memphis, Tennessee

Mother addicted to crack

Has turned to prostitution at times

Baby born with breathing trouble and heart defect.

Or -

Baby born to white college professor parents

Born in New England,

A brother to two twin sisters,

Born in the best hospital in the area,

A healthy nine pound baby.

The inclusion of the racial difference between these two children is not an assumption on my part as to the desirability of either skin colour. It is a statement on the advantages such a child will have being born into their societies in that physical form under those conditions. How much harder will it be in the circumstances for a black female to grow up poor and sick in the South of the U.S.A than for a white male in a middle class world? If one were to add that the first child was born in the nineteen fifties in the South then the circumstances would be even more highly stacked. And the odds against her rise, the further back in the twentieth century that she is born. Why would a soul wish to opt for that poor female when they could choose the parents that would bring forth a fine privileged male?

This question brings us back to one we have encountered before...why bother to incarnate at all? In this case why bother to incarnate and have a rough deal when you could have a nice manifest ride, enjoying the fruits of the material world? Well, let us look at example two, the middle class and healthy boy. There could be many, many reasons to come to incarnation as this character and only one of those reasons is to have a comfy trip through life. Sure, some incarnations we can take a breather and learn some lessons without being the underdog or the victim. Sometimes we can learn just as much whilst sitting on a favourite armchair than on a hard wooden bench! One does not need cushions in order to be creative or a thinker or a carer or a teacher but sometimes having those cushions can be nice! Especially if for the last few incarnations you chose to learn from war, poverty or injustice at first hand. Lets face it, comfort in the world is not a bad thing! It should be everyone's right. The fact that it isn't is part of the reason that we are all incarnate. Taking our male example then, let us take some for instances branching from his cosy start to life. Maybe then -

a) The boy is good and appreciative and learns to pass his excellent fortune on to others by way of voluntary work. He could use his wealthy background to travel overseas and do aid work. He could study at University and go into a profession which would help the same people who were not as lucky by birth as he. He could use his status to be heard as a respected campaigner for human rights. In short, he uses the life wisely as a way of growing in compassion.

b) The boy could be apathetic, lazy and indifferent to all he has been given by birth. He could be careless at school, thinking that his parents would always bail him out anyway. His intelligence was not as abundant as his material good fortune and no amount of schooling or money could change this. He felt rebellious against his fathers relentless pushing of him academically when he would rather be goofing around on the sports field. Having no interest in much besides himself and his gratification he was cold or abusive to more intelligent, less attractive school pupils. He could get involved at a young age with drinking and soft drugs, having a large allowance to spend as he wishes,. In such a state he could drive a friends car into a wall and fatally injure the passenger whilst becoming paralysed himself. From his enforced position of stillness he could reconsider his attitude and be thankful for his own life and disgusted with himself for killing his friend. His struggle to make amends and to show his sorrow and repentance would be to tour schools talking to young adults about what had happened to him, advising them of the dangers of such substance abuse. He uses the second part of this life as a way of teaching others whilst learning to cope with being disabled. He is not capable of supporting himself in the manner to which he had been lead to believe was his right by birth and so learns to deal with disappointment, frustration and regret.

c) The boy does indeed have a wonderful childhood but during adolescence his father has an affair with a student, who he gets pregnant. His mother, who has herself entered the menopause, becomes greatly disturbed and begins drinking heavily. During her rages at being left alone, she beats her teenage son and vents her anger at his father upon him. She loses her teaching job and his two older sisters are forced to leave home, without their higher education being completed, to find work. The son, feeling guilty and out of love for his mother, misses his own chances in order to look after and support her. In this life, the son enjoys a degree of material comfort only to have it taken away by someone else's mistakes. He learns to see how lying and violence are not solutions and how ones own irresponsible actions can have far reaching affects. He learns to be selfless and how to be supportive, things that would not necessarily have been understood if he did not have the confidence that his happy and secure earlier years had instilled in him.

From these three sample scenarios we can observe;

a) How many and varied are the learning experiences that could come from this birth option.

b) How the birth option did not guarantee that the others involved in it would behave with any degree of reliability, no matter how idyllic the setting. Therefore we can see the webs of the connection between all souls in a particular set of circumstances. We can see how one action can affect much more than just the person committing the action.

c) We can see the choices and the use of free will, or of inherent soul qualities, which make the best, or the worst, of given life circumstances.

d) No two souls would react the same way in the same set of circumstances. Therefore each soul would learn entirely different things from each life environment, or manifest situation.

The pre-birth choice of who we are going to be and in what set of circumstances has an infinite amount of outcomes, depending on a blend of that individual soul, the people playing alongside and of the lessons that need to be learned or shared from it. Remember, the group soul ethos is about collective learning and so their may be a gathered consensus about a birth scenario in order to get as much from it as possible.

At the end of the day, the souls free will, choice and personal traits will either come through to triumph over adversity or to be defeated by it. Maybe, indeed, the lesson could even be about wasting a life, indifference or missed opportunities. The race, gender, abilities, size and physical characteristics of the body we inhabit have as much to influence the set of circumstances as any other factor. There is an endless list of combinations of these things which make for subtle shifts in the matrix of energies which are our lives here on earth. How we, and how others, perceive the flesh vehicle can be a huge issue in an incarnation. It is what we have set out to understand through this perception that is important. Ultimately, we could be anyone, as long as that someone fulfils the criteria for a valid learning experience.

Soul is neither racist nor sexist, religious nor bigoted, fanatical nor tyrannical. These are human qualities, brought on by circumstance, indoctrination, other abuses or fear. Soul is not evil nor is it wholly good. Soul just is, a unique and particular blend of subtle energies, looking to get better at being that soul. Incarnation is the thing that makes us act our roles, for better or worse, but always with a point or purpose. There is no act of cruelty or abandonment which does not have a reason. However, even to one who has conscious recall of other lives (far memory) the reason can be a long time in becoming clear. Of course, the soul itself knows the reason and purpose of all actions. Yet the manifest persona, even if it exhibits the sensitivity and psychic sight to recall other lives, may not grasp such patterns for many lifetimes.

I myself have been given the ability to remember and see my other selves, my alternative personas or characters in other times. I do not believe that everybody can do this, although I have, luckily, met other people who can. One knows a far memory as much as a memory from this life, perhaps a distant childhood memory. All soul memory has a distinctly personal feel to it, this feel has an emotion attached to it. We do not remember every time that we sat on the toilet, or washed the dishes, (unless such things give you an emotional response!) as there is no great feeling of sadness, love, regret etc. to make it valid to store. Such memories are deep within us but if they were all readily accessible on a daily basis our heads would be full to the point of discomfort. So it is with far memory. If we could all remember all of our other lives, here in the now then we would be confused and our systems constantly overloaded. We need that distance and a feeling of belonging in this place and time. Only those who spend time involved with psychic work or research have the focus or the space to accommodate the selective recall of other life times. Other peoples heads are more occupied with their own accumulated knowledge relating to their professions and interests. That is how it should be and is appropriate to their incarnate self, neither way being right or wrong, only different.

Within the soul, all things are recorded and can be accessed. As a natural psychic, my meditation work takes me to a place where I may examine and explore my other lives quite easily. I find that when I need to understand something vital about myself, or others, with reference to my own work and development, then the memory surfaces anyway. For example, when I needed to know why I was getting more and more phobic about burning myself and being nearly hysterical with fear at the thought of being near fire I remembered the circumstances in which this terror began. I did not need to relive them, merely to examine key points in an old life pattern. It is crucial to remember in all other life recall that it is the pattern that is important not the minutiae.

I had been burned in 1326, in Avignon, France. I had been a midwife who lost a woman and her child and had been seen, because of this, as an evil witch. I had been burned at the stake next to the one man I had ever loved, who would not acknowledge me. With that one recollection came the understanding of the fire phobia (irrational in twentieth century England, but not to my scarred soul which bore the trauma) and also my distaste for childbirth and children generally (I felt afraid of them as if they could hurt me somehow). I did not need to relive the burning. I just needed to see the pattern and to acknowledge it. I also needed, at that point, to meet the man I had loved in that life. We needed to meet again in this incarnation to go through the patterns of loss and grief and on his part, guilt. We had unfinished soul-business together. The fire phobia had heightened so that the memory would be triggered. From the memory came the understanding of the situation that was occurring in this life with the man who I had loved in 1326.

The man that I was with had his own individual, separate memories of that life we had together. He could fill in the gaps where I could not remember, or from times when we had not been together. Such was the power and potency of his own recall that he had been afflicted with blisters and sores, equivalent to those that he would have had in the first stages of burning. Such was his own souls trauma that his bodily or manifest self actually simulated the burning scars. This condition passed as he dealt with his own deep feelings, at a soul level, about such an act of brutality which was completely unjust and had been for no good reason. He in that life had been an itinerant healer and had wandered from place to place administering his skills on the needy in return for food or clothing. He is, in this life, a healer and psychic and so his past life recall skills were to the fore. He had remembered the burning incident as part of his own process of self-discovery and meditation.

The fated way in which we met and the intense connection that our souls had lead us to believe that we were exclusive soul mates. Not so! Time revealed to us that we were just meeting again as kindred spirits from the same soul group or type to resolve our shared soul hurts. We were able to love each other through the grieving process of letting go of the anger, fear and pain of such a soul experience. We completed the unfinished business of being a partnership, something that had been curtailed so horrifically by the authorities in 1326. We were able to help each other with the phobias and hang-ups, both about societies injustices and about our own eternal selves. Then we moved on from each other as we both understood on a psychic soul level that we had other people to meet and work with and other lessons to learn.

This meeting of two people who have the ability to share spontaneous other-life recall is unusual. Most recollections do not come through with such clarity, especially not for both people involved. As we were both engaged in that line of work and research then we both had the ability to process and accept such memory. In my experience, people that I have shared life-recall with have either only had a vague feeling or a fragmented vision of our previous connection. Sometimes they even have a completely different memory of the events, although they know they were there and that I was there too. That deep feeling inside which accompanies a genuine memory was there for them even though their recall differed from my version of events.

As an example, a partner of mine had known me in several lives, two of which were clearer than the rest. We both agreed that we had known each other in World War One and that it was very resonant as a chord between us. Neither of us had a great knowledge or fascination of that time period but we were, none the less, soul-connected to it, and to each other. Yet he had recalled me as his wife who stayed on his farm when he went to war...whilst I saw us both in the trenches as close male friends, young and frightened. I even saw myself at the moment of my death, being blown up by an explosive. So, we both acknowledged the profound feeling of connection to the war and to each other but in completely separate ways.

Again, when we both agreed that we had been together in England at the time of Richard the Lionheart, he saw himself as a farmhand whilst I saw him as a horse trainer. The memories of the other circumstances of the life fitted together but our perceptions of the actual details differed. Why?

Sometimes a memory only sees what it wants to. We are quite capable of re-writing history in our own personal lives when looking at past situations. We tend to embroider or to cover up those bits which do not sit right with our consciences. Indeed, the perception of the same event by five different people would be coloured by their own personal preferences, previous experiences and personalities. Therefore one would probably get five different reports of the same event.

Similarly, when a test was done with several witnesses watching a simulated crime, the view of the suspect varied enormously based on these same personal traits. The patterns may stay the same but the details are coloured by our own vision of the world. This is why it is only the patterns which are relevant, whilst the incidentals (name, place, date, costume, etc.) are transient and unimportant... just props in the life-drama.

Is this a cop out which is all but admitting that past, or other, life memory is nothing but a fraudulent fantasy? When two people cannot tally up on details in a recall, but can remember the same key events doesn't that mean that it is all, in effect, so much rubbish? As another example, recently I watched a documentary on the immensely talented late singer/songwriter Nick Drake, who died tragically as a depressed and isolated man.

The programme used a group of different acquaintances and professional contacts of Drake to compile a complete picture of the man. Although they had been at the same concert or at the same event, their personal recollections of how Nick Drake behaved was totally different. They could all state categorically that they were there at the theatre, their memories of the key moments were in tandem. Yet their view of the man himself could be as diverse as remembering him withdrawn and unwashed, with horrendously long fingernails, to quite optimistic and chatty. This was a memory of an event which happened in the 1960s....not hundreds of years ago! Still, the recollections of any group of people will differ on the minutiae, not on the bigger key moments.

It is, to the serious student of the mysteries of death and rebirth, only the patterns that matter. They tell us all that we need to know to understand who we are and why we are here. This does not mean that past life memory cannot sometimes be historically validated, in an amazing way. In my own experience, I had been suffering from a recurring nightmare which was getting more frequent. It involved a tiny room with a wooden window. It was a room that held a lot of confusion and fear for me, which had no correlation to my life now but in which I was trapped. I decided to seek help to explore this obviously important, though difficult, part of me. During a session of guided meditation, I remembered a life as a monk in an Abbey called Welbeck, in England. I was able to describe events in the abbey concerning a particularly devious and crooked Abbot. I was also able to follow myself through to my untimely death, which occurred in the small room of my dreams. I had tried to speak out for justice against the Abbot and he had me hunted down and killed by a soldier. The soldier used a peculiar type of weapon, which I saw clearly in my recall.

On coming out of this very vivid and personal soul-memory (it moved me to tears) I was able to discover that Welbeck Abbey had indeed existed and had recorded problems with a very unsavoury corrupt Abbot, which lead to its eventual dissolution. This was a small, obscure Abbey which no longer stands and one which I had to look up in many specialist volumes in order to discover its presence at all. Similarly with the weapon, the dates I had remembered for my lifetime then coincided with the use of a particularly nasty looking lance or bayonet style item...exactly the one I had seen and subsequently sketched out. The times before and after my life had used quite different looking spear-headed weapons.

As an example, I think that my own experience shows how personal validation of historical facts can help us to give credence to our own memories. The minutiae of that existence was lost but the crucial points...the weapon that killed me, the Abbey that housed me...stayed stuck fast in my mind. I have no specialist knowledge of medieval weaponry or of Britain's monastic dwellings. It is these things which lead me to believe in my other more vague recollections. All real memory feels the same to me, it resonates personally on a soul level. Having the occasional historical validation just adds weight to the belief in the whole process of past life research for the purpose of personal growth. I do not expect such facts to arise on every occasion and neither should anyone who is genuinely curious about their own other existences.

Another example of historical validation comes from *More Lives than One?* by Jeffery Iverson (Souvenir, 1976). This is an interesting book which is still extremely orientated in the proof aspect. Recall and lives which are at all sketchy are felt to be not as valid as the ones that provide concrete evidence of a researchable nature. It is, however, excellent in the fact that it provides transcripts of the six different past-life recalls of one woman. From this, a study of the patterns occurring with the persons soul could be studied and the book could have progressed in a much more questioning way. However, its role was to prove reincarnation by fact. I have not time here to recount all of this woman's recollections (and doubtless she had dozens more lives to remember, these being the most important ones to her at that time) but I will recommend the text for anyone who would like to independently study the purpose and patterns of a clutch of incarnate lives such as these. They do indeed provide a bigger picture of the purpose of the soul of the lady involved. Much more can be learned from the collective pattern than from getting bogged down in the accuracy of historical fact. When one bears in mind that history is, yet again, a fallible documentation written by a handful of men who coloured things with their own viewpoints, it should not have too much emphasis hung upon it. The actual feelings of the soul concerned are far more valid indications of the spirit of those times in which it lived on earth.

In one particularly emotive recall, this lady recounted a life as Rebecca of York in the year 1189. The history around this time and area is not that clear and so when the woman came up with memories involving having to wear a badge that signified her religious origin it was impossible to state if this was correct or not, only possible, knowing the feel of the times. The woman, as Rebecca, describes a wealth of family detail leading up to the third crusade, yet it is the emotional involvement of her soul with this particular set of events which shines from her words. This was not a woman weaving a fantasy from threads of historical knowledge...and even if, by some chance, it were, the emotional connection that her psyche feels with that era must mean something relevant to her soul-nature.

Even if we study far memory and recall as nothing but soul-fantasy, not a truth, then we still see the same patterns and connections of feeling and being that tell us definitive and profound things about the soul.

The woman, as Rebecca, goes on to recall a man whom she recalls as Mabelise, an enemy of the Jews and one who illicits a passionate negative feeling in Rebecca. It would be churlish to discount her memory of this man because she mispronounced his name...it was, in fact, Malebisse. She continues with her soul-story, becoming increasingly distressed as she tells of hiding with her family against the riots which rage. The people of York were full of an anti-Jewish fervour which lead to them discovering Rebecca and her hidden loved ones in order to kill them. Before the death of that character, the woman/Rebecca recounts her story in a voice incoherent with terror. The characterisation which was directly expressed in response to the questions of the interviewer (a professional person trained to take people back into their far-memory) and could not be so instantly contrived. Further sessions revealed Rebecca of York to have an entirely different personality to that of the woman who was remembering in the now.

The outcome of the research into this life of Rebecca was that if the woman had wished to pick a remnant of fact for fictionalisation into a character/story then she could have found much less obscure references. A professor, a man with published work on the time involved in the recall, stated that the information given ranged from being impressively accurate to something which could well have been true. In other words, some of the key material was probable, whilst the minor points were possible. However, the most exciting and substantial piece of truth gleaned from the intensely personal far-memory of the woman was that subsequent excavation of a small church (the one in which Rebecca claimed to have been hiding). During this excavation they found the very crypt that she had stated she was in. Previously, there had been no evidence of any such church with a crypt in that vicinity. The very fact that it was not found until after her recall is one which gives immediate credence to her tale. Although on a soul level, one needed to have looked no further than the genuine emotions involved in order to see the real meaning of this recall, fantasy or not.

So, how may one experience a recall, how may you the reader experience accessing your own far memory? There is no need for regression-hypnosis, only for a relaxation and meditation/visualisation which is easily achievable (with the right focused intentions). This should be preceded by asking yourself the following question;

What do I most need to know, at this time, about my souls pattern?

This could be with reference to -

a) Nightmares or recurring dreams which affect you personally and cannot be readily dismissed.

b) Any fears or phobias which affect your life currently and do not relate directly to an event in this incarnation.

c) Any relationship problem or pattern which cannot be broken easily and which comes back again and again.

d) Any passionate pulls that you feel to a particular area or person or interest which are getting stronger.

This list is by no means conclusive and should be expanded by questioning your individual needs in the now. Remember... this is not an opportunity to watch a good film of yourself in another guise, this is a focused exercise and the more you can do prior to the event, the more connected to its purpose you will feel. It is helpful and sensible to keep a journal or record of your feelings and thoughts for at least a week before entering into this exploration of the soul. This journey should be done as part of an overall quest, not as an isolated incident with no meaning nor any conclusion. Try and make it a part of your ongoing voyage of self, or soul, discovery.

This work, or recall, will not -

a) Give clairvoyant/psychic advice such as "you should leave your partner tomorrow". It will not act as an instant fix to sort your life out.

b) Involve any loss of free-will or consciousness. It is not a mind-manipulation and has no hold over you. You are at liberty to come and go as you please from it, with full authority.

When you have cleared your intentions and made notes on what you hope to set out to achieve, then you need another aid...a trusted friend or colleague with some understanding of the process. If they have none to begin with then at least make sure that they have a sympathy or interest in the subject matter. It must be someone you trust due to the intimate nature of the material that you may or may not come across. They will not be actively involved in the process other than talking you through it. In time, this process may be worked through with several people at once, as long as there is always a trusted person in the room who is not part of the memory experience. Someone must remain objective and separate and act as a watcher, someone who will time the activity and talk the participant/s in and out of it. They may also need to provide drinks, tissues or a listening ear afterwards. Remember, this is actually quite hard, intense work, not a game. Make sure that you are fit, alert and relaxed at its start...or do not proceed. This cannot be rushed under poor conditions.

Now return to chapter two and become fully conversant with the relaxation/protection ritual which must precede any act of soul-work. Do not proceed without a thorough grounding in this matter...it is vital and to consider it less than vital is akin to stepping blindly onto a motorway. Psychic work needs protection. Similarly, you will need to fully ground yourself after the session and be completely returned to the now so ensure that you re-read the information on grounding in chapter two.

You should be relaxed, lying down with a pillow under your head and a blanket around your body is usually appropriate. Comfort is not distracting whilst cramped limbs and cold feet are! You may like a tape recorder running on a long play cassette as to have a record of the proceedings. Have your friend instruct you to relax and visualise protect-ion for yourself. You may indicate to them when you have completed this task. Then they will slowly and thoroughly lead you through the following steps -

a) Imagine yourself in a summer meadow on a pleasant day. Stand still in the long grass which is filled with a riot of wild flowers and fill your minds eye with the scene around you. Take in the blue sky and the shape of any passing clouds. Feel the warm breeze and smell the scent upon it. See the hills and trees that surround you on all sides. Hear the whisper of the grasses and the song of the birds. Then notice before you a trackway made by a wild creature in the grass. Follow it.

b) The trackway will take you into a wooded area and you can see its progression through the ferns and plants on the floor. Notice the change of light and smell as you walk beneath the trees. In a moment you reach an ancient and knotted hollow oak which stands directly in your path. Feel awe at its age and venerability. Put your hands onto the bark and feel the roughness. Then notice that there has been a low arch formed in the hollow centre of the trunk. If you duck down you may creep through the centre of the hollow tree. It is a tight squeeze but you manage to get through to the other side. Touching the bark again you offer thanks and move on.

c) Again on the trackway you notice that a small stream has cut across your path. Reach down and cup a handful of clear water to wash your face. See the small silver fish darting past. You may cross this stream by stepping on three flat stones. Count them and be careful of their slippery surface as you cross. Hear the bubbling water behind you and move on.

d) Take a few more steps and see before you a grassy bank which you will need to climb. You cannot see over it. You press your hands to the rich earth and smell the soil. Scrambling up you peer over the top.

e) Before you in a clearing stands a building. This building must come to you directly. Do not think rationally of any meaning, rather just see the first shape or form that comes to you. Take a few moments to see the place that you have imagined. See its windows and the shape of the roof, the colour of the bricks and the type of chimney stack. Now climb right over the bank and down into the clearing. The building stands before you waiting and inviting you in.

f) You stand before the house and study the door, its size, colour, texture, door handle etc. Know every detail before you approach it and push it open. It is open as it has been expecting you and you alone.

g) You enter the house and are standing in an entrance hall. See any items that may be present there and note if there are any stairs or doorways. Focusing on your purpose for exploring your other lives, consider whether it is most appropriate for you to go up, or down, the stairs or through a doorway. Again, do not dwell on this for meaning, act on instinct. Go with whichever option feels appropriate. Count the stairs as you go or see the door as you push it open.

h) Having gone up or down stairs or through the doorway (being careful to observe the details of both) see that you are now in a room which has a door on each wall. Note the floor, the colour of the walls and the nature of the doors. Again, dwelling on your purpose, consider which door to choose on this occasion. when you have chosen, go through it. It will lead you into the correct life for that question.

i) At this point, you may be flooded with images. If so, remain calm and still and take stock of exactly what is going on in front of you. Perhaps you have just stepped into darkness, in which case, remain in place and get a sense of self. In either case breathe steadily and slowly and begin to focus on your being. Firstly look down on your feet. Can you see them? Do not try to consciously think of what they look like, rather pick up any feelings or sense of what you have on your feet. If you are not able to see immediately the pay particular attention to the feelings involved. Do you feel strong? Tall? In pain? Happy? Different at all? (N.B. If no image or feeling comes within a few minutes then go back through the door and retrace your steps carefully through the house and outside. Go back until you are in the meadow again. Then gradually picture yourself back in the room you are in. You have not failed, this just isn't the right time. Maybe you are tense or tired? If so, try again another day, do not worry, it is best not to rush or get frustrated if nothing is happening naturally.) If you can get a sense of self and even start to see your hands, feet and clothes, then excellent! Flow with the images and feelings, do not take time to rationalise them as this will kill spontaneous recall. It is hard, at first, to quell the conscious rational mind, this skill comes with time and practice.

j) If you have a sense of appearance then focus on who you are...what is your name, who are you in the community, how old are you, where are you, what are you doing? If you can answer these questions without allowing that voice of reason to creep in and analyse your feelings then you are doing very well indeed! Allow the first thing that comes to mind to be the thing you say. Allow the images to form around the question and see yourself stepping into the scene further, into the role or the drama. Keep tuned in to feelings of being in a new body, a different self or persona. Describe what you can see and let any other information flow from it.

k) Allow yourself to focus on the purpose of your visit. What is it that you have come to find out? Allow time to adjust to your self and the environment and then look at what you are being shown around you. Who is there? What are you doing? Why? Where? Is anyone speaking? (The person/friend in the room who is guiding you should keep you focused and on task but allow a good ten minutes for this exploration. A few key questions to keep in touch with you should act as triggers to memory. If the guide sees you are becoming distressed it is up to them to ask you to leave before this conn- ection grows too strong. They are your link to the now and their voice is your beacon in this strange 'new' environment. Remember, you are not hypnotised, only deeply relaxed. You can come back into the room at any time. It is best to do this slowly, retracing your steps, but if necessary you can leave immediately, provided you ground yourself adequately afterwards and talk through your experiences in full. See chapter two for grounding skills.)

l) Once a ten minute observation of the scene and events has been completed it is advisable to leave. It is best to do several short sessions rather than one mammoth one, especially on the first attempt. The guide should gently ask you to come back through the door, leaving the experience behind you when the door is closed. This is important as a portal of the self is effectively closed and no after-effects can be brought back into the now. The slow and methodical retracing of steps can take place into the meadow and from there back into the room.

m) This may be replaced at point e) by the appearance of a flying machine/beast/bird...anything from a U.F.O to a pterodactyl which can carry you into the sky. You approach it and either climb inside or onto its back. Again, take time to make this real by seeing texture/colour/form clearly. This flying transport has to be real (in your imagination or third eye space) for it to be safe! Once aboard you are taken up and away. You may see all sorts of scenes beneath you, landscapes, cities, sea, desert. Focus on the question in hand and tell the flying transport to land at the place most appropriate to this question. Once you land, take in the scene before you as you would at point i). When you are ready to leave (as you would go back trough the door) get back into/on this mode of fantasy transport and come back to the bank of earth and the clearing. Then retrace the steps as with the other technique.

n) Ground yourself fully and thoroughly after each session.

Make notes of everything that you learned initially from this session. Were you surprised to see yourself as male when you are now female, with different coloured skin maybe? Did you expect to find yourself in the role of victim, yet discovered yourself as an attacker? This can be rather shocking, to discover that your soul had once portrayed the aggressor, in bodily form. Knowing that such roles are never just for the hell of it should make it easier, if initially you are rather alarmed by this you. As I said in my book *Wildwitch* (Capall Bann, 1999) I had once gone into a mediation and discovered myself as a male who had raped. This was, of course, abhorrent to the now me and I wondered how my soul could do such a thing. I guess the answer to that is that it had to, due to its circumstances, to understand the full horror of what a man was capable of. I am sure there were a thousand other lessons and reasons for committing such an act, all based on bigger patterns, circumstances and influences. I do know that it would never happen again and that I truly accepted the lesson, on all levels. I also accept full responsibility for my actions.

The truth is that when you walk through the door into the relevant life, you could be anyone! It matters not who you are now, that will pass away. Your soul will clothe itself in any array of garments, in any location. Did you feel that sense of surprise on some level as you noted which disguise your soul was wearing in that life? Or did it feel entirely natural to you, even though it was different to what you know in this life? As you go into such questions and soul-searching, you will probably remember more information or see more imagery connected with that life-pattern. Now you are open to its possibility with a welcoming spirit then the images may come through unhindered. Be prepared for this to happen and keep a note of any feelings, however vague. Everything is important at this stage. Later you may become more accomplished at weeding out what is frippery from what is key material.

Were you shocked by the level of emotion you felt in this 'stranger's' body? Did you see something affecting or unpleasant.? Chances are that you did, as you would not be drawn into a banal or ordinary life memory when you had specifically been after a key issue. If one does an unfocussed, tourist style journey into any old random existence then one maybe could expect chaff. The case of the man who was stuck in a past-life scenario of "trimmin' the hedge" springs to mind! This is a good example of why not to waste time day-tripping into incarnations. He had gone into his past lives for fun and had ended up at random in a tedious setting!

If you did chance upon a deeply affecting scene then you can work with it. Changing the past, by working through fear, loss, anger, etc. is possible. I myself have returned to the 'witch burning life' in order to confront those who chose to obliterate my life force, which offended their blinkered view, in the most torturous way. I did not dwell upon their evil, they were only misguided characters living lives which were affected by the combined might and crushing weight of the church and state. They probably lived in their own fear, as was the desire of the establishment of the time, using fear to control the masses.

I have never sought to have revenge upon my tormentors, nor have I ever wished to meet them again. They were only minor characters playing their role in a soul-play, the pattern of which was my own victimisation and persecution for being unusual. However, this did not stop me from wanting to enter that reality and to change it on some level. If one opens up to the possibility of past lives being other lives on different levels of existence then it is perfectly feasible to travel through these layers of existence and to alter them, making yet another reality.

To do this, I entered the other-life realm that I had focused on, (namely Avignon town square, set with three stakes) using the above technique. Instead of passively watching the events, I decided to actively intervene with the knowledge of my soul and of my current 'me' to guide me. I did not enter the scene to hurt or kill but to rebel and say "no". Consequently, I was able to visualise my chopping up the crude wooden stakes and casting them into a fire. I was able to address my attackers face to face with eloquence far beyond the capabilities of that poor medieval midwife 'me'. I was able to break my bonds and walk free from them.

This was extremely liberating. It means that on some level, that was reality, that was a possible outcome. In linear time, my witch burning still exists as fact, but in possible other realms or dimensions, it never was. The conclusion of this book deals with this concept more fully but here I will say that on whatever level, the act of taking control and personally changing a situation is very therapeutic. The same could be said about visualising oneself as a child again and imagining what you would say to those schoolroom, or playground, bullies, given the full weight of knowledge and understanding of your adult self. This does not mean retribution, only re-addressing the balance. It is an act of positive will, and a method of soul-healing. "I could do something" is far more uplifting than "I could do nothing".

Now that you have begun your own journey, a personal and unique voyage into soul discovery, you have had your own glimpse at the truth. This is your truth, be that a soul-fantasy or not. Although one should be open to change and possibility, the personal truths to be discovered in the past or other life arena are pretty much eternal and unshakeable. They are born of the soul and the soul, as we have observed, is all there is after the temporary illusion of the manifest has passed away again.

Your soul is more than just what you wear today, or how much money you earned last year. Your soul is you beyond death. As you have seen from your initial work with that eternal spirit, it can robe itself in many 'flesh mantles'. The only preference of the universe is that the mantle be appropriate...be it considered ugly, poor, noble or radiant.

As you may have observed from your soul-journey, you can recognise another familiar, or kindred, soul by the eyes, by the vibration. Not by the colour of the hair or size. No soul is inherently blue eyed with golden hair. These are temporary trappings. The soul is that which shines out from the eyes, be they brown, be they behind glasses, be they almond shaped with heavy lids. If you meet another kindred soul in this life, or in your journeying, be sure to connect with the eyes and the vibration of a touch. Not by the confusing outer garments. This person may have been a limping leper the last time you met them and now they are a fashion conscious hairdresser! Look beyond, look inside.

Once you begin this questing journey you will change. There will be more understanding. With understanding comes compassion. With compassion it is only a short step to realising, we can be one another yet remain inherently what we at our very centre of being. The soul-song remains the same but the harmony or rhythm alters. In incarnate life, we can indeed be one another, in all eternity we can be pure soul. It is the acceptance of this potential which can open us up to each living thing on this beautiful planet. It is the experience of being open to feeling emotion in another persons shoes that the study of 'other lives, other selves' offers us. Not only this, but exploring the patterns of incarnation can lead us to truly know who and what we are, inside, and to really rejoice in that adaptable, yet eternal energy that we uniquely are. We are as organic as the earth, as infinite as the universe and growing towards our own inherent, and singularly special, best.

We are now, we have been and we will be again. It is ours to do with as we will for the good of ourselves, and so consequently for the benefit of the All. This book has offered

108

the opportunity to work with this eternal self consciously in an effort to understand our nature and our patterns of potential. It is my hope that you will be inspired to do so...the quest is your own.

Conclusion

Other Realities?

This chapter really should have begun with this line... "Many worlds at once? Some patterns of possibility." However, it was already spoken for, used as a hypothetical title for a lecture in Richard Bach's superb book *One* (Pan, 1988). This book is a perfect example of how the questing mentality of a soul open to new ideas is inspirational in itself. Mr Bach is one who is filled with joy at the personal understanding that he does not know...but oh the excitement of trying to know!

His brave dealings with concepts that are fashioned from an intoxicating mix of science and esoteric thought are chronicled in the book. On reading his words it is his infectious enthusiasm, lack of fear or judgement and his patient attempts to understand which truly make the reader open up to wholly new horizons...even when some of them are almost too baffling to contemplate. Richard Bach takes a very complex and difficult train of thought and makes it palatable to anyone who lacks an scholarly and academic mode of processing information...a rare talent.

The book *One* explores the many lives/many selves model of reincarnation, only from an angle which suggests that maybe this is all happening in the now. Therefore it is a model of incarnation, as all lives are happening simultaneously, only in different guises, places, times etc. Not only is time not linear but it is also multi-layered, a three dimensional object in itself. Time could be seen, perhaps, as overlapping tracks on the skin of an orange, a sphere of continuing time, round and round, crossing over and moving on. Similarly, the web of fate could be seen as a tree which branches and branches again, shoots and roots eventually curling around to meet each other.

Once again, coming at this as a pattern of possibility rather than a concrete fact or an utter nonsense, we can consider that whilst we enact one strand on the web of fate, our counterparts in other dimensions take the other, less defined, less obvious paths. Maybe they do so to test it out on your behalf? Maybe they are not as valid as you? Or maybe they are just different, equally relevant parts of a whole self?

Maybe one such part of your self had the accident that you narrowly avoided as a child? Maybe they married the woman who you turned down and had a wonderful relationship? Maybe they never recovered fully from the food poisoning that you got over three years ago and so their health is impaired? Maybe they accepted that hit of heroin that was offered to you in the 1970s...

All of these possibilities that you, the you on this level, did not take, they did take. That means that their lives are parallel maybe but they lead off in other ways. As your life does to them. Your grades at school took you to a certain University whilst theirs didn't. Your footballing career was terminated by injuries whereas theirs wasn't. As an idea, this means that we can experience most things simultaneously, now, in a multi-layered way. Again, at its most basic this could be seen as a case of good self/bad self... or successful self/failure self, and so on.

However, the possibilities are, as usual, far wider and more far-reaching than such simple delineations of self. For example, there is a matter of finding a lost purse. In one reality, one 'you' hands it over to the Police untouched. In another, one 'you' takes the money out but hands the purse in. In yet another version, one 'you' only takes five pounds from the purse and hands the rest of the money in, whilst one 'you' does not want the hassle and kicks the purse under a bush. Possibly another part of you may take all of the money and credit cards too.

So, all of your potential selves have a bit of that stupidity or intelligence within them. Maybe their mix of these attributes is just different to your own. Maybe their circumstances causes that mix of attributes to become imbalanced. The self who lived in a shack in South Africa would respond differently to the one who studied at Sarah Lawrence in North America. The potential you in a village in India may have been, in essence, the same as a you who works in an office in Hong Kong but the circumstances of the life twist and stretch those base qualities. This is learning, and there is no differentiation between a good or a bad lesson. As we may realise by now, different is no better, no worse.

In this simultaneous manner, you could learn all the life lessons at once and recoup all the knowledge on the point of death (when presumably the soul reunites with all of its fragmentary parts and shares what it has learned as a whole being.) Perhaps, then, we can also consider that whilst the person we are now is engaged in a myriad of scenarios coming from the same fated route (or root), yet another soul-fragment is living out a life in Renaissance Italy, another bit in thirteenth century France, another fragment in Poland in the Second World War and so on.

Indeed, perhaps we do not come back at all, in a linear sense. Maybe our dejá vu experiences are due to us experiencing the same set of circumstances over and over until we learn? Maybe we see these circumstances as being gilded with Japanese details or the trappings of an Innuit lifestyle. Maybe the whole costuming and staging of these life dramas is nothing but a projection onto the same set of soul-players?

To say 'past lives' makes us seem as if we are progressing along a trackway towards something. What? It surely cannot be enlightenment of a universal kind as we have looked at the unlikely nature of this blanket sort of perfection. We have assumed, because we have had to order ourselves into morning/ afternoon/ evening, home/ work/ social life, birth/ marriage/ death etc. that one life follows from another in an equally orderly line of progression.

However, we have looked at the possibility of us learning as being the only reason for incarnate existence. If this is so then we can consider that most usually we learn from reading a book, chapter by chapter, building up a clear picture or following instructions. We do not tend to dip in or jump pages if we wish to be thorough. Yet we know that not everyone is academic and that the universe allows for different talents and skills and ways of being. Again, the analogy of a fly being different, but no less valid, than an elephant. Nature accommodates the strangest of beasts over a period of time and evolutionary distance.

Perhaps, then, nature will accommodate for those who learn in a more fluid way. Perhaps a more hands-on approach, more practical, or more creative and random? Therefore, is it not a possibility that some of us prefer to incarnate on multi-levelled now existences whilst some of us like to plod from one time period to the next, learning directly from the last life in the line?

Neither or both responses may be correct. It is the sheer suggestion of this possibility that is exciting and stimulating on a personal level, at least. I myself love the idea that I am currently leading a life as a singer somewhere, with the long hair I always wished for. That me took chances that I never did. Yet that me could not write this book and is probably too busy to even consider sitting and pondering such huge, ultimately unanswerable, questions. Yet as they are a part of the root me then they must have a bit of my spiritual curiosity. Maybe it is expressed as a discreet Buddhist philosophy or an occasional foray into a Christian church? Maybe that me cries at the Catholic Christmas mass? Maybe another me is a man born of my parents on my birthday, getting a male perspective for my soul on living at the close of this century. Maybe! It is all possible.

I love this idea. As Edie Brickell, the American songwriter/ vocalist, married to Paul Simon, once sang "somewhere there's a person who looks just like you do, acts just like you too, feels the same way, somewhere there's a person in a faraway place with a different name and a face that looks like you...do you think about who it might be, do you wonder where you are, in a distant foreign country, riding round in another car...where the wheel keeps on turning and turning..." Maybe that person is in this world with me now, a doppelganger placed at the other side of the globe from this 'me'. Would it be in our line of learning if we were to meet?

What would you say to the other 'you' if you could step into their life? Would it make you realise that you couldn't judge anyone for what they did, what they thought or believed? If you saw yourself in another life making different choices would you finally understand how we can all do certain things under certain circumstances, that no one is fully bad, that we are, essentially, one another?

Reincarnation is no more than a soul-resurgence, a renewal, a movement involving growth. It may be a progression through an ordered view of world history, it may be the multi-layered experience of our soul-pieces in different realities, it may be a continuum with different settings and costumes but the same characters. Perhaps reading this book has helped you decide which sounds like the most comfortable possibility to you. Or, better still, you will have been inspired to put together your own model of possibility for incarnate being?

What if, though, this is all rubbish? What if! It is a possibility, after all. Does it matter? We can at least feel happy that we know by understanding that we do not know. Yet if the ideas and suggestions in this book have made you think, consider, question or change then this in itself is enough. The concept and possibility of reincarnation was enough.

And if this book made you kinder, more aware, less ready to judge or condemn then it was worthwhile.

Fear and ignorance as regards the unknown are the only cause of disharmony and hurt. We see this as evil, in its extreme manifestations. If this simple, yet profound, set of possibilities help to consider that everything is connected in a variety of ways and therefore to hurt another wilfully is to hurt the self, then they are not rubbish. They may not be universal truths but if we can hold on to them as personal ones then we at least will be living as if we truly are one another.

With this one leap of consciousness, this one step of faith and with the hard work and effort that goes with letting go of old and comfortable notions then we may really be kind spirits. Past, present and future, on all levels of consciousness, this will be felt as a gesture of love. It cannot fail to be felt.

We are one another.

Soul Resurgence - A Guide to Reincarnation by Poppy Palin

This book explores the possibility that the soul is the 'eternal self', or spirit essence, which has the capability to travel through incarnate life cycles in a 'flesh vehicle', or human body. It looks at the nature, origins and purpose of soul in comparison to the bodies or masks that it chooses to wear whilst 'in the world'. *Soul Resurgence* contains simple techniques and methods for the reader to gain their own personal understanding of both their own eternal self and the reasons why it has chosen various bodily guises through time. Reincarnation is discussed in terms of it being a renewal or movement towards growth as opposed to a linear ascension into a universally defined perfection. The purpose of becoming incarnate in order to learn how to become the best sort of soul that you can be, given your type, is put forward as the central issue. It is a book which promotes new ways of seeing our own unique part in the web of existence, stemming from the spiritual premise "we are one another". ISBN 186163 1162   £7.95

Season of Sorcery - On Becoming a Wisewoman by Poppy Palin

"fascinating...stunning...very nice pathworkings...all this without losing her sense of humour! An extremely interesting book" Greenleaf

Many people experience psychic phenomena to a greater or lesser degree, depending on their own innate sensitivity. Such experiences can cause delight or distress and can be difficult to share with others. This book is a personal story of psychic encounters, and the author's own understanding of them, presented as a fascinating blend of information and entertainment. In sharing her own unusual experiences, the author hopes to encourage others to gain knowledge and understanding of their own. The book therefore seeks to inspire by revealing the author's own practical understanding and enjoyment or her own psychism and encouraging the reader to develop and understand their own. ISBN 1898307 96 2   £10.95

Wildwitch - The Craft of the Natural Psychic by Poppy Palin

Explores the energies of the Wild, the natural world, and working with them for positive, harmonious results. *Wildwitch* encourages the reader to rejoice in their own inherent psychic ability and to use it with integrity and wisdom including working with Other Realms, spirit and the personal Guide. Poppy's experiences are used to illustrate and bring to life the points made. *Wildwitch* advocates progressing along a very individual spiritual path, encouraging the reader to explore the wilderness within and without, accessing the hidden places and looking for truths where others do not. This book's roots are firmly in the tradition of the Craft, but it also looks deeper, using questions as part of the reader's quest, encouraging individual thoughts, answers and truths. *Wildwitch* is, essentially, about the energies that link us all, incarnate or in spirit, written from the perspective of one who works with these energies as a way of life. ISBN 186163 103 0 £10.95

FREE DETAILED CATALOGUE

Capall Bann is owned and run by people actively involved in many of the areas in which we publish. A detailed illustrated catalogue is available on request, SAE or International Postal Coupon appreciated. **Titles can be ordered direct from Capall Bann, post free in the UK** (cheque or PO with order) or from good bookshops and specialist outlets.

Do contact us for details on the latest releases at: **Capall Bann Publishing, Freshfields, Chieveley, Berks, RG20 8TF.** Titles include:

Angels and Goddesses - Celtic Christianity & Paganism, M. Howard
Arthur - The Legend Unveiled, C Johnson & E Lung
Astrology The Inner Eye - A Guide in Everyday Language, E Smith
Auguries and Omens - The Magical Lore of Birds, Yvonne Aburrow
Asyniur - Womens Mysteries in the Northern Tradition, S McGrath
Beginnings - Geomancy, Builder's Rites & Electional Astrology in the
    European Tradition, Nigel Pennick
Between Earth and Sky, Julia Day
Book of the Veil , Peter Paddon
Caer Sidhe - Celtic Astrology and Astronomy, Vol 1, Michael Bayley
Caer Sidhe - Celtic Astrology and Astronomy, Vol 2 M Bayley
Call of the Horned Piper, Nigel Jackson
Cat's Company, Ann Walker
Celtic Faery Shamanism, Catrin James
Celtic Faery Shamanism - The Wisdom of the Otherworld, Catrin James
Celtic Lore & Druidic Ritual, Rhiannon Ryall
Celtic Sacrifice - Pre Christian Ritual & Religion, Marion Pearce
Celtic Saints and the Glastonbury Zodiac, Mary Caine
Circle and the Square, Jack Gale
Compleat Vampyre - The Vampyre Shaman, Nigel Jackson
Creating Form From the Mist - The Wisdom of Women in Celtic Myth and
    Culture, Lynne Sinclair-Wood
Crystal Clear - A Guide to Quartz Crystal, Jennifer Dent
Crystal Doorways, Simon & Sue Lilly
Dragons of the West, Nigel Pennick
Earth Dance - A Year of Pagan Rituals, Jan Brodie
Earth Magic, Margaret McArthur
Eildon Tree (The) Romany Language & Lore, Michael Hoadley
Enchanted Forest - The Magical Lore of Trees, Yvonne Aburrow
Eternal Priestess, Sage Weston
Eternally Yours Faithfully, Roy Radford & Evelyn Gregory

Everything You Always Wanted To Know About Your Body, But So Far
    Nobody's Been Able To Tell You, Chris Thomas & D Baker
Fairies in the Irish Tradition, Molly Gowen
Familiars - Animal Powers of Britain, Anna Franklin
From Past to Future Life, Dr Roger Webber
Gardening For Wildlife Ron Wilson
God Year, The, Nigel Pennick & Helen Field
Goddess on the Cross, Dr George Young
Goddess Year, The, Nigel Pennick & Helen Field
Goddesses, Guardians & Groves, Jack Gale
Handbook For Pagan Healers, Liz Joan
Handbook of Fairies, Ronan Coghlan
Healing Book, The, Chris Thomas and Diane Baker
Healing Homes, Jennifer Dent
Healing Journeys, Paul Williamson
Healing Stones, Sue Philips
Herb Craft - Shamanic & Ritual Use of Herbs, Lavender & Franklin
In Search of Herne the Hunter, Eric Fitch
Intuitive Journey, Ann Walker Isis - African Queen, Akkadia Ford
Legend of Robin Hood, The, Richard Rutherford-Moore
Lid Off the Cauldron, Patricia Crowther
Light From the Shadows - Modern Traditional Witchcraft, Gwyn
Lore of the Sacred Horse, Marion Davies
Magical Guardians - Exploring the Spirit and Nature of Trees, Philip Heselton
Magical Lore of Animals, Yvonne Aburrow
Magick Without Peers, Ariadne Rainbird & David Rankine
Masks of Misrule - Horned God & His Cult in Europe, Nigel Jackson
Medicine For The Coming Age, Lisa Sand MD
Medium Rare - Reminiscences of a Clairvoyant, Muriel Renard
Menopausal Woman on the Run, Jaki da Costa
Mind Massage - 60 Creative Visualisations, Marlene Maundrill
Moon Mysteries, Jan Brodie
Mysteries of the Runes, Michael Howard
Mystic Life of Animals, Ann Walker
New Celtic Oracle The, Nigel Pennick & Nigel Jackson
Pagan Feasts - Seasonal Food for the 8 Festivals, Franklin & Phillips
Patchwork of Magic - Living in a Pagan World, Julia Day
Pathworking - A Practical Book of Guided Meditations, Pete Jennings
Personal Power, Anna Franklin
Places of Pilgrimage and Healing, Adrian Cooper
Practical Divining, Richard Foord
Practical Meditation, Steve Hounsome
Practical Spirituality, Steve Hounsome
Psychic Self Defence - Real Solutions, Jan Brodie
Real Fairies, David Tame
Romany Tapestry, Michael Houghton

Sacred Animals, Gordon MacLellan
Sacred Celtic Animals, Marion Davies, Ill. Simon Rouse
Sacred Dorset - On the Path of the Dragon, Peter Knight
Sacred Grove - The Mysteries of the Forest, Yvonne Aburrow
Sacred Geometry, Nigel Pennick
Sacred Nature, Ancient Wisdom & Modern Meanings, A Cooper
Sacred Ring - Pagan Origins of British Folk Festivals, M. Howard
Season of Sorcery - On Becoming a Wisewoman, Poppy Palin
Seasonal Magic - Diary of a Village Witch, Paddy Slade
Secret Places of the Goddess, Philip Heselton
Secret Signs & Sigils, Nigel Pennick
Spirits of the Air, Jaq D Hawkins
Spirits of the Earth, Jaq D Hawkins
Spirits of the Earth, Jaq D Hawkins
Talking to the Earth, Gordon MacLellan
Taming the Wolf - Full Moon Meditations, Steve Hounsome
Teachings of the Wisewomen, Rhiannon Ryall
The Other Kingdoms Speak, Helena Hawley
Tree: Essence of Healing, Simon & Sue Lilly
Tree: Essence, Spirit & Teacher, Simon & Sue Lilly
Understanding Chaos Magic, Jaq D Hawkins
Vortex - The End of History, Mary Russell
Warriors at the Edge of Time, Jan Fry
Water Witches, Tony Steele
Way of the Magus, Michael Howard
Weaving a Web of Magic, Rhiannon Ryall
West Country Wicca, Rhiannon Ryall
Wildwitch - The Craft of the Natural Psychic, Poppy Palin
Wildwood King , Philip Kane
Witches of Oz, Matthew & Julia Philips
Wondrous Land - The Faery Faith of Ireland by Dr Kay Mullin
Working With the Merlin, Geoff Hughes
Your Talking Pet, Ann Walker

FREE detailed catalogue and FREE 'Inspiration' magazine

Contact: Capall Bann Publishing, Freshfields, Chieveley, Berks, RG20 8TF